spring 2014

Mission

We understand "community literacy" as the domain for literacy work that exists outside of mainstream educational and work institutions. It can be found in programs devoted to adult education, early childhood education, reading initiatives, lifelong learning, workplace literacy, or work with marginalized populations, but it can also be found in more informal, ad hoc projects.

For us, literacy is defined as the realm where attention is paid not just to content or to knowledge but to the symbolic means by which it is represented and used. Thus, literacy makes reference not just to letters and to text but to other multimodal and technological representations as well. We publish work that contributes to the field's emerging methodologies and research agendas.

Subscriptions

We are pleased to offer subscriptions to CLJ—two issues per year:

Institutions & libraries	$200.00
Faculty	$30.00
Graduate students & community workers	$20.00

Please send a check or money order made out to the University of Arizona Foundation to:

John Warnock, *Community Literacy Journal*
445 Modern Languages Bldg., University of Arizona, P.O. Box 210067
Tucson, AZ 85721
Info: johnw@u.arizona.edu

Cover Art: "Artisanal Expertise: Wool Dyeing in Lurín, Peru" by Aida Villarreal-Licona

Aida Villarreal-Licona, Scripps College 2016, Media Studies and Spanish, served as a summer Media Intern and Photographer for emiLime Handcrafted and Green Design Link, companies that connect artisans in Peru with the global marketplace. This photograph was taken at the home of master weaver Urbano during a wool-dyeing workshop attended by his wife Teodora and their friend and fellow artisan Juan Carlos in Lurín, Peru. It captures the near-end result of the dyeing process after wool has been spun and soaked in boiling plants, such as molle and chilka, and minerals including iron and copper sulfates. The literacies circulating in these workshops range from cross-generational, to botanical, to artisanal and historic, as the pre-Columbian techniques that are used have been learned, passed down, and practiced in these artisans' families for many generations.

Editorial Advisory Board

Jonathan Alexander	University of California, Irvine
Nancy Guerra Barron	Northern Arizona University
David Barton	Lancaster University, UK
David Blakesley	Clemson University
Melody Bowdon	University of Central Florida
Tara Brabazon	University of Brighton, UK
Danika Brown	University of Texas–Pan American
Ernesto Cardenal	Casa de los Tres Mundos, Managua
Marilyn Cooper	Michigan Technological University
Linda Flower	Carnegie Mellon University
Diana George	Virginia Tech University
Jeff Grabill	Michigan State University
Greg Hart	Tucson Area Literacy Coalition
Shirley Brice Heath	Stanford University
Tobi Jacobi	Colorado State University
Lou Johnson	River Parishes YMCA, New Orleans
Paula Mathieu	Boston College
Regina Mokgokong	Project Literacy, Pretoria, South Africa
Ruth E. Ray	Wayne State University
Georgia Rhoades	Appalachian State University
Mike Rose	University of California, Los Angeles
Tiffany Rousculp	Salt Lake Community College
Cynthia Selfe	The Ohio State University
Tanya Shuy	National Institute for Literacy
Vanderlei de Souza	Faculdade de Tecnologia de Indaiatuba, São Paulo
John Trimbur	Worcester Polytechnic Institute
Christopher Wilkey	Northern Kentucky University

spring 2014

COMMUNITY LITERACY *journal*

Editors	Michael R. Moore DePaul University
	John Warnock University of Arizona
Senior Assistant Editor	Amanda Gaddam DePaul University
Copy Editor	Edward Evins DePaul University
Journal Manager	Daniel James Carroll DePaul University
Design & Production Editor	Aim Larrabee DePaul University
Book & New Media Review Editor	Jim Bowman St. John Fisher College
Social Media Editor	Melissa Pompos University of Central Florida
Consulting Editors	Eric Plattner DePaul University
	Stephanie Vie Fort Lewis College
	Rachael Wendler Univerity of Arizona

Submissions

The peer-reviewed *Community Literacy Journal* seeks contributions for upcoming issues. We welcome submissions that address social, cultural, rhetorical, or institutional aspects of community literacy; we particularly welcome pieces authored in collaboration with community partners.

Manuscripts should be submitted according to the standards of the *MLA Handbook for Writers of Research Papers*, 7th ed. (New York: MLA).

Shorter and longer pieces are acceptable (8–25 manuscript pages) depending on authors' approaches. Case studies, reflective pieces, scholarly articles, etc., are all welcome.

To submit manuscripts, visit our site—communityliteracy.org—and register as an author. Send queries to Michael Moore: mmoore46@depaul.edu.

Advertising

The Community Literacy Journal welcomes advertising. The journal is published twice annually, in the Fall and Spring (Nov. and Mar.). Deadlines for advertising are two months prior to publication (Sept. and Jan.).

Ad Sizes and Pricing

Half page (trim size 6X4.5)	$200
Full page (trim size 6X9)	$350
Inside back cover (trim size 6X9)	$500
Inside front cover (trim size 6X9)	$600

Format

We accept .PDF, .JPG, .TIF or .EPS. All advertising images should be camera-ready and have a resolution of 300 dpi. For more information, please contact Michael Moore: mmoore46@depaul.edu.

Copyright © 2014 *Community Literacy Journal*
ISSN 1555-9734

Community Literacy Journal is a member of the Council of Editors of Learned Journals

Printing and distribution managed by Parlor Press.

spring 2014

COMMUNITY LITERACY Journal

Volume 8 Issue 2 Spring 2014

Table of Contents

Articles

Reframing the Argument: Critical Service-Learning and
Community-Centered Food Literacy 1
Veronica House

Assembling for Agency: Prisoners and College Students
in a Life Writing Workshop 17
David Coogan

"Socializing Democracy": The Community Literacy
Pedagogy of Jane Addams 33
Rachael Wendler

Investigating Adult Literacy Programs through Community
Engagement Research: A Case Study 49
Jaclyn M. Wells

Reading Under Cover of the Veil: Oral and Textual
Literacies in Antebellum America 69
Sandra Elaine Jones

"To Learn About Science": Real Life Scientific Literacy
Across Multicultural Communities 81
Adriana Briseño-Garzón, Victoria Purcell-Gates, and Kristen H. Perry

Book and New Media Reviews

From the Book Review Editor's Desk 109
Jim Bowman

Keyword Essay: "Community Management" 110
Jennifer deWinter

*Unsustainable: Re-imaging Community Literacy, Public Writing,
Service-Learning and the University*
By Jessica Restaino and Laurie JC Cella, eds. 117
Reviewed by Jody A. Briones

*Cultural Practices of Literacy: Case Studies of Language, Literacy,
Social Practice, and Power*
By Vicoria Purcell-Gates, ed. 121
Reviewed by Kelly A. Concannon Mannise

Local Literacies: Reading and Writing in One Community
By David Barton and Mary Hamilton 126
Reviewed by Charlotte Brammer

Literacy in the Digital Age, 2nd edition
By Richard W. Burniske 129
Reviewed by Lilian Mina

Re-Framing the Argument: Critical Service-Learning and Community-Centered Food Literacy

Veronica House

As a WPA and a service-learning director and practitioner, the author suggests connections between food studies, rhetoric and composition studies, and critical service-learning theory that involve mobilizing students to join in or help lead community efforts surrounding the local, organic food movement, food justice, and food literacy. The study is framed by questions of how composition instructors can create courses around issues related to the global food crisis to embed students in community-centered food literacy initiatives, and, more generally, how practitioners and WPAs can effectively promote and explain community-engaged pedagogies to higher-level administrators who question the value of the practice.

I recently had a conversation with a dean at the University of Colorado Boulder about why the Program for Writing and Rhetoric made a curricular commitment to service-learning and civic engagement throughout its lower- and upper-division courses. More specifically, he wanted to understand the benefits of service-learning for students. He was not interested in assessment data about personal growth and civic learning. That students become more engaged and "critical citizens for a participatory democracy" (Berlin 97), as has been shown in numerous large and small-scale assessment studies (Ash, Clayton, and Atkinson; Astin and Sax; Eyler and Giles; Eyler, Giles, Stenson, and Gray), did not particularly impress him. "Yes," he said, "but is there something about service-learning that teaches students more effectively *how to think and write*?"

As some within Rhetoric and Composition Studies argue to move beyond Paula Mathieu's "public turn" to a "political turn"[1]—one that would focus more deliberately on political issues than the social turn of the 1990s—practitioners, scholars, and WPAs once again face a host of questions that get at the heart of why we teach and what higher education's purposes are and should be. This is nothing new. These conversations have persisted through the last century from John Dewey to Paulo Freire to Ernest Boyer. In Rhetoric and Composition specifically, binary viewpoints about how to teach and the purposes for rhetoric and composition classes incite emotional and compelling arguments. In one camp, for example, are critical literacy scholars such as Henry Giroux and Ira Shor, who argue that critical pedagogy is an "emancipatory" project of "transformative intellectuals" (Giroux 174-175). Critical pedagogue James Berlin declares, "the objectives of English Studies are many. *The most significant of these is developing a measure of facility in reading and writing practices so as to prepare* students for public discourse in a democratic political community (Berlin 110, emphasis added). For the "first-wave" critical literacy pedagogue, the primary purpose for teaching writing is neither to prepare students for academic life or the workforce nor to help them express themselves more clearly (Seitz 506). Rather, it is "as a political and moral project ... [to] illuminate[] the relationships among knowledge, authority, and power" in order to prepare students for civic life (Giroux "Critical Interview"). Because of its "consideration of ideological issues," which may also "foreground awareness of social and political inequalities and consideration of ways to resolve them," critical pedagogy is often linked with teaching for social justice (Durst 3).

On the other end of the spectrum, Stanley Fish boldly proclaims to fellow academics: "Save the world on your own time," in his 2008 book by that title. In the first of his three 2009 *New York Times* editorials on the subject of composition pedagogy, he writes, "How can I maintain [...] that there is only one way to teach writing? Easy. It can't be an alternative way of teaching writing to teach something else (like multiculturalism or social justice)." He declares that academics who do the latter are "not doing the job."

Between the extremes, a rich body of scholarship addresses the complexities and paradoxes in critical pedagogy. Criticisms include the fear that an overtly political or "critical" pedagogy forces students to adopt the instructor's viewpoints or "reinforces relations of domination," (Yoon 729; Ellsworth; Gale; Lynch), can ironically be "disempowering" for students (Gallagher 78) and is a pedagogy of affect that seeks to shame faculty who do not adopt a critical framework (Yoon). These "post-first-wave" scholars, as Paul Feigenbaum calls them, focus their discourse "on implications of the challenge itself rather than possibilities for cultivating critical consciousness"[6].

Others argue for a balanced approach. Russel Durst posits in his qualitative study on the effects of critical pedagogy in composition classes that instructors should mediate between their desire to teach politically-charged material and the students' desire for instrumentalist instruction that will help them gain jobs after graduation. He urges "the preparation of students *as writers* within the context of the field's social turn," or what he calls a "reflective instrumentalist" approach (6, 177-178, emphasis in original). In a similar vein, in his discussion of James Berlin, Joseph Harris argues that while critical pedagogues advocate "a shift in focus *away from the practice of writing* and toward questions about social values, subjectivities, ethics, and ideologies," he urges "a renewed attentiveness to the visible practice or labor of writing. My aim in doing so is not to depoliticize the teaching of writing but to suggest that our first job is to demystify the actual workings of academic discourse" (577-582, emphasis added). Durst discusses "a strong tendency now in composition studies to focus almost exclusively on ideological matters ... but it is not immediately clear how they map onto our role as teachers helping our students to improve their writing" (5). In other words, many scholars fear that writing instruction is obfuscated when the course is themed around politics, cultural issues, or social justice.

In light of this discussion on the benefits and detriments of incorporating politics and social justice issues into composition courses, I would like to return to my dean's question about the value of service-learning as a pedagogy, for his concerns seem to stem from a similar place as those vocalized by critics of critical pedagogy. Although service-learning might seem like the next, even more radical step beyond classroom-based critical pedagogy, it may, when executed well, offer answers to many of the above concerns. The fact is, these need not be black and white choices about education and pedagogy. We need not choose between teaching for the public good and teaching for rhetorical awareness, genre understanding, or skills acquisition. Nevertheless, my dean's question is an important one that represents the many questions that we must be ready to answer, from those within and outside of our discipline, if we are to encourage continued support for and funding to service-learning programs and courses.

The persistent misconception that service-learning is simply touchy-feely, non-academic, volunteer work threatens the endurance and proliferation of the pedagogy. When it comes to service-learning's purposes and outcomes, to borrow Linda Adler-Kassner's terms from *The Activist WPA*, we must more effectively shape and control the "frames"[2]–the narratives surrounding service-learning and community-based pedagogies (37). While I agree with those who argue for a socially conscious curriculum, I fear that to foreground an overtly political approach may not be supported at many institutions and, therefore, may deter colleagues—particularly those on the tenure-track—from teaching service-learning courses. I also take K. Hyoejin Yoon's criticisms about critical pedagogy seriously in relation to service-learning. This kind of pedagogy should not be about "affect"—about posturing or shaming colleagues who are not equally "enlightened" in their pedagogical choices. Service-learning is a pedagogy that enhances learning. Period. In this article, I use the community-based food literacy projects from three service-learning rhetoric and composition courses as models for reframing the conversation in order to enable the durability of well-constructed service-learning courses[3].

Getting to the Root of Food Literacy

Before I discuss the three food literacy projects in detail, I'll give a bit of context for why I teach food-themed rhetoric and composition courses. In short, the American food system is in crisis. The way most Americans eat is a major contributor to climate change and environmental, economic, and cultural degradation. The industrial food system is dependent upon fossil fuels for chemical fertilizers and pesticides and for "planting, harvesting, processing, packaging, and transport[ing]" (Brownlee 2). While straining to meet the food demands of the growing world population, our food system is implicated in causing and perpetuating hunger and disease in the United States and abroad, and these problems are likely to worsen as the price of oil rises. Our methods for growing food are destroying our topsoil and contaminating our waterways. Large multinational corporations such as Monsanto and Nestle seek to control the world's access to food and water. As people have been de-skilled over the last half-century, "our communities can no longer feed themselves" (Brownlee 4). As our food system has changed to feed people ever more "cheaply," our population, surging under this never-before-seen access to cheap food, is growing exponentially at an unsustainable rate (Bartlett). Quite simply, we cannot sustain infinite growth on a finite planet.

Because of all this, one could argue that colleges and universities have a responsibility to teach students about our flawed food system. Many research-oriented universities have not traditionally seen teaching courses related to agriculture or farming as part of their mission, but as climate change and peak oil loom, so does the need for more universities to expand their scope and re-envision their mission. As Derek Owens argues in *Composition and Sustainability*, "A sustainable society cannot be created without sustainability-conscious curricula" (27).

"The food revolution," as it is called by many members of the movement, that is taking root in communities across the country, is branching into academic disciplines under the umbrella term "food studies," which includes "historical, cultural, behavioral, biological, and socioeconomic" approaches to the topic (Nestle 160). What began as a social movement is fast becoming an academic movement with food studies majors, graduate programs, conferences, and academic journals popping up around the country. I suggest connections between food studies, rhetoric and composition, and service-learning that involve enhancing students' ability to think and write critically about the systemic, root causes of societal problems by mobilizing them to join in or help to lead community discussions surrounding the local, organic food movement, food justice, and community-centered food literacy. By taking this approach, we provide a powerful learning experience for our students that is emotionally and intellectually complex, while at the same time offering opportunities for the students to work toward social change through writing.

In Boulder, CO, where I live and teach, there is an active, visible push on campus, in the city, and in the surrounding communities toward re-localization of the food system, which means moving toward local production of food and goods to support local economies and to decrease our dependence on fossil fuels, agribusiness, and factory farms. A purpose of the food re-localization movement is to educate people, as a kind of cultural literacy, about the origins and contents of their food and about the systems that they support with each purchase. Another purpose of the movement—because approximately 34,000 people, or 12% of the population of Boulder County, are food insecure—is to empower, through knowledge and skill building, disenfranchised members of the community who cannot afford to purchase healthy, organic food (Brownlee 17, 19). The goal is for our community "to meet [its] essential needs locally, and in the process to become more resilient and self-reliant" (Brownlee 1). Because food sovereignty and food justice are some of the most important issues of our time, issues that tie to topics of ecological collapse, peak oil, racism, poverty, corporate capitalism, overpopulation, disease, and hunger, service-learning practitioners are well-positioned to help launch initiatives in colleges and universities across the country, in partnership with our local communities, to address community-centered food literacy.

In the following pages, I examine how current theories of service-learning can help mobilize composition instructors to create productive service-learning projects that center on campus and community food literacy and food justice in order to enhance students' writing and critical thinking abilities. I address the following questions: How do we create purposeful assignments that will involve students on the front lines in local communities? How do we teach community-based genres that can intervene in public discourse? How might practitioners and WPAs "frame" this work for audiences less interested in the civic learning goals of the course or literacy work in general?

Traditional and Critical Service-Learning

In current service-learning scholarship, a distinction has emerged between traditional service-learning and what is now called *critical service-learning* (Mitchell; Cipolle). Traditional service-learning is a form of experiential education that integrates academic instruction and regularly scheduled critical reflection with educationally meaningful community-based work that is appropriate to curricular goals in order to enrich and enhance the learning experience, teach civic engagement, and meet community-defined needs (adapted from the National Commission on Service-Learning). As Susan Benigni Cipolle explains, however, "while there are many worthwhile service projects that meet real needs in the community, for service-learning to be *critical*, students and teachers need to examine issues of power, privilege, and oppression; question the hidden bias and assumptions of race, class, and gender; and work to change the social and economic system for equity and justice" (5, emphasis added). Following critical service-learning scholar Tania Mitchell's lead, I address below, "How might the curriculum, experiences, and outcomes of a critical service-learning [composition] course differ from a traditional service-learning [composition] course?" (50).

In the first several weeks of an upper-division food-themed rhetoric and composition course that I teach at the University of Colorado, students read about the issues of the food movement and complete assignments such as a comparative rhetorical analysis of readings and an inquiry paper. In the much-echoed trilogy of service-learning, these assignments help ground students in the "What?" and "So what?" questions that will ultimately move them to the "Now what?" question. During this phase, students visit the non-profit sites a few times to get a feel for the environment and meet some of the staff and clients. In the article's next section, I will discuss two community-based food literacy projects, one at an after-school program for at-risk children and another at a day shelter for Boulder's homeless and working poor, and one campus-based food literacy project.

For the service-learning component of the course at this early stage, students may help tutor children at the after-school program or serve meals at the shelter to begin to understand how the non-profit operates. This is traditional service-learning at work, and if it were all students did with the partner organization, their experiences could potentially reinforce previous stereotypes and the social status quo. While students begin to make connections between their readings, research, and community-based observations, they are not yet performing work with a "goal, ultimately, [...] to deconstruct systems of power so the need for service and the inequalities that create and sustain them are dismantled" (Mitchell 50). This is a distinction between traditional service-learning and critical service-learning. But perhaps this distinction is as much about critical thinking and well-constructed courses as it is about a social justice mission for education.

Assignments and discussions in all service-learning courses should help to move students to the "Now what?" phase, but how to do so? I have written about the Reflective Course Model in which I adapt Sarah Ash and Patti Clayton's DEAL Model for Critical Reflection (House). As part of their critical reflection model, they ask students to answer the following questions: "What did I learn? How did I learn it? Why is it important? What will I do because of it?" (Ash and Clayton). Teachers and students evaluate the reflections based on ten critical-thinking standards such as accuracy, clarity, depth, and fairness, established by the Foundation on Critical Thinking. In my Reflective Course Model, I suggest that we embed Ash and Clayton's reflection questions into all writing assignments so that the course itself becomes a kind of meta-reflection that moves students through the series of questions as the semester progresses. Students use the critical-thinking standards to revise their work. The second half of the course, then, becomes the embodiment of the "Now what?" or "What will I do because of it?" question.

Here is where social justice work can result, not as an instructor's imposed political or ethical agenda, which is a major criticism of both critical pedagogy and service-learning, but rather, as a necessary conclusion to any carefully designed theme-based service-learning course whose learning goals include critical thinking[4]. Within the timeframe of the course, students will enact answers to Ash and Clayton's final reflection question, guided by critical-thinking standards.

I suggest that we revisit the "critical" in critical service-learning as a conflation of critical pedagogy, which is the intended reference, with critical thinking. When students make the leap from studying manifestations of a problem to analyzing systemic, root causes, they move toward a critical understanding that better lends itself to informed action, the "What will I do because of it?" I am reminded of Ira Shor's students standing at the river's edge, "toes in the dark water," who contemplate at the end of Shor's course how to cross over into "organized action for change" (177). Service-learning helps guide students across the deep river. Mitchell explains:

> [a] recent study by Wang and Rodgers (2006) shows that a social justice approach to service-learning results in more complex thinking and reasoning skills than traditional service-learning courses. A critical approach embraces the political nature of service and seeks social justice over more traditional views of citizenship. This progressive pedagogical orientation requires educators to focus on social responsibility and critical community issues. Service-learning, then, becomes "a problem-solving instrument of social and political reform" (Fenwick 6, qtd. in Mitchell 51).

This idea of "problem solving" is compelling. When we talk about teaching—some might say preaching—"social responsibility" or "engaged citizenship," we can find ourselves in a messy territory where accusations of agenda-pushing liberalism fly (Harris 577). As Paul Feigenbaum explains, "[c]ritical teachers ... invariably trap themselves (and students) by imposing social visions rather than creating dialectical opportunities for reflection and action" (10, original emphasis). Well-constructed service-learning courses create those dialectical opportunities.

While certain audiences will acknowledge the importance of civic learning goals, others, like my dean, will not. Practitioners and scholars must be ready with other arguments. Mitchell stresses, "a critical service-learning approach allows students to become aware of the systemic and institutionalized nature of oppression" (54). This growing awareness, however, is not about students feeling good—or bad—about themselves. It is not about providing charity work. It is not about an instructor's political or ethical agenda. Rather, when we shift the focus to intellectual rigor, problem solving, critical thinking, and higher-order reasoning, all of which lead to enhanced writing, we make the connection to academic learning outcomes and begin to change the "frame" or narrative.

Well-constructed theme-based service-learning courses immerse students in complex rhetorical debates and community conversations to teach them how to use writing, genre knowledge, and rhetorical strategies to make something happen. This may or may not be a moral or ethical decision on the part of the instructor, but of more importance, it challenges students to think critically and to deeply explore, challenge, and subvert the systemic, root causes of the manifested problems they see.

Figure 1, filled in by my students during a classroom lesson, delineates the students' understanding of issues at an after-school program in Boulder, where they worked to develop a comprehensive nutrition program.

The figure illustrates the ways in which students can develop deeper understanding as they become more aware of the complexities of the issues with which their non-profit

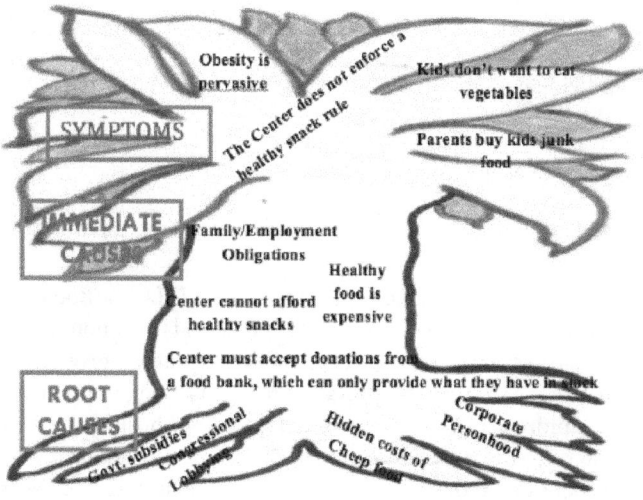

Figure 1[5]

wrestles. Initially, students recognize the symptoms, indicated in the leaves of the tree. If students are not encouraged through assignments and discussions to delve into the causes, they may spend their time at the non-profit entrenching previous stereotypes and generating inaccurate assumptions (Bringle and Hatcher 84, Ash and Clayton 26). On the other hand, if they are encouraged to investigate the immediate and, eventually, the root causes of the symptoms, they become ready to answer "Now what?" or "What will I do because of it?" in a more informed and substantive way. Therefore, social justice issues enter the classroom alongside students' developing knowledge, which grows out of research, readings, and experience, all viewed through the lens of critical thinking standards. Instead of distinguishing civic learning from academic learning[6], the two become inextricable from one another, which strengthens the argument for the social justice element of the course, not as an ethical obligation, but as an academic necessity. It's where students end up when they think deeply about the issues.

How To Do "Critical" Work Through Community-Centered Food Literacy Initiatives

I offer three class projects as examples for moving beyond a service-learning model that might reinforce the status quo to a "critical" model that encourages students to use critical thinking and problem-solving skills to enable change in the community. In my courses, learning objectives mirror traditional composition course goals established by my program but include additional goals that a student will learn to:

1. balance theory and research with analysis of community-based experiences

2. recognize and analyze correlations between theoretical concepts and community experiences

3. produce writing that effectively responds to or addresses a community need

4. distinguish individual manifestations of a problem from the systemic, root causes

5. assess rhetorical circumstances in the public sphere and intervene appropriately through writing and civic action

6. create purpose-driven documents for audiences beyond the classroom

In a class project with the Family Learning Center (FLC), a Boulder-based non-profit whose mission it is to provide learning skills that lead to economic self-sufficiency for children and families of limited incomes (FLC website), University of Colorado students worked with the elementary program to help develop a comprehensive nutrition program for the children. FLC families struggle to afford healthy food, and children come to the center with their favorite snacks of raw ramen noodles, "hot" Cheetos, and Coke. University of Colorado students learn, through readings and research, to trace the "symptoms" that they see at the FLC to root issues, such as the government's subsidy policy for grain crops; corporate personhood; and systemic, deliberate failings to provide affordable nutritious food to our country's poor. "Now what?" they then ask. What might they as a class do because of these "learnings" to help the FLC families to decrease dependency on the industrial food system, gain sovereignty over their food, and become food literate—objectives that the FLC elementary program director and my students determined to tackle?

Group projects grew out of this challenge. One group set out to teach the FLC children how to garden. As one group member, Raven Emmons, wrote in a critical reflection assignment,

> In the context of food security, reskilling, and community integration, group (or community) awareness is truly our first step in beginning a cycle of change and growth. The point of the FLC garden is to open the gate to healthy, locally-grown food as well as provide a sense of community for underprivileged, under-recognized youth; in essence, we are fighting many social norms and structures that contribute to these people's subjugation, which requires attention to the subtleties, a higher level of commitment to the project than what is typical in the university, and, I daresay, passion!

The group wrote letters to local farms and hardware stores to request donations of seed, soil, and supplies for the elementary garden, which the group went on to plant with the FLC kids. The children could share the garden's produce with their families, thus becoming responsible for helping to feed their own community.

To help ensure the sustainability of the project, the garden group produced two manuals, one for children and one for future University of Colorado students who will take over the garden project in subsequent semesters. Thinking through the lessons they learned about purpose, rhetorical appeals, and audience awareness, they produced a fifteen-page laminated, brightly colored guide for the eight- to ten-year olds, filled with pictures and easy-to-understand language about maintaining and harvesting the garden through the summer and fall. The more technical, 50-page "Garden Handbook" for future groups of college students contains detailed sections on garden program elements ranging from topics such as "Soliciting Donations," "Preparing the Soil," and "Companion Planting."

A second group wrote and designed a 75-page cookbook with and for the children and their families that includes the children's favorite food memories and family recipes made healthier by my students. It includes an introduction in which the writers tailor, to the education and knowledge level of the FLC parents, the lessons they learned throughout the semester on problems with the industrial food system, childhood obesity, healthy habits, the re-localization movement, and the need to re-skill children in the pleasures of gardening and cooking. The cookbook could be given to the children and sold by the FLC at fundraisers.

To address issues of parental food literacy, another group wrote a weekly newsletter for FLC parents—translated into Spanish by a staff member at the center—about nutrition and food access in Boulder County. The students researched food access organizations to determine alternate ways in which families could attain healthy food—produce in particular. The nine newsletters that they produced cover wide-ranging topics such as "Fast Food and Restaurant Nutrition for Kids," "Healthy Snacks," "Cash Saving Tips," "Organic Versus Non-Organic," "What are GMOs?," and several stories about the garden and cooking projects the FLC kids did with University of Colorado students. As with the cookbook, the challenge was to tailor arguments and suggestions, which in initial drafts were too complex and academic, to a low-income and often semi-literate audience, in order to educate and persuade them to change engrained habits and to seek alternate methods of accessing and preparing food.

The learning that took place for the fourth group, specifically, involves a kind of complexity that would not have been possible in a traditional classroom. Perhaps surprisingly, the most significant demonstrations of enhanced learning did not explicitly connect to the thematic material of the course, e.g. the readings and research on food, but rather, to the rhetorical strategies that we studied alongside the thematic content. The fourth group wrote lesson plans for and taught healthy-eating classes and science experiments involving food. While the enthusiasm in the group was high, students quickly learned that audience is key when creating arguments. When the group initially met with the children, they prepared a lesson on nutrition, talking to the eight- to ten-year olds about vitamins, nutrients, and how parts of the body are affected by various vegetables. The kids were bored. Fidgets and whispers quickly devolved into full-fledged chaos. My students were frustrated and felt that the task was too daunting. Over several weeks of trial and error, however, they were able to tailor their arguments about nutrition to their young audience, and the classes became more hands-on, visual, and effective.

The group realized that if they had been given an assignment in a traditional composition course to produce hypothetical lesson plans, they, and I, would have assumed that they would be successful. The service-learning experience forced them to drastically re-think their approach to teaching the FLC kids, and through that process, it also deepened their understanding of the applicability of rhetorical principles in complex, "lived" experiences. The cooking group produced a dozen lesson plans and a fifteen-page resource guide for future University of Colorado students. In their introductory letter to future students who would use the guide, they wrote:

> Context, purpose, and audience are extremely important in writing your lessons. It is crucial to recognize your audience so that you can effectively reach them… Pathos, logos, and ethos are important to incorporate into lesson plans and activities. You must gain credibility so the kids trust you and believe the information you give them.

The guide delves into these broad rhetorical concepts in detail. Through these community-based food literacy projects, the University of Colorado students and the FLC elementary director hoped to lay a foundation for healthy lifestyles and ways of unplugging from the industrial food system for the FLC children and their families.

What none of the students anticipated, but all learned, is the essential nature of the rhetorical and genre analyses we practiced during the first month of the course in terms of writing in community contexts. When they misjudged their various audiences, did not provide appropriate context, did not understand the nature of the genre in which they worked, or did not, themselves, have clarity of purpose, the documents failed. An extensive revision process, which included several conversations with FLC staff, parents, and students, helped to ensure that the final products met their intended goals.

Another class worked with the Bridge House, a non-profit organization that aids Boulder's homeless and working poor. The Bridge House received a grant to purchase a commercial kitchen, which promised to fundamentally shift the way in which they offer food to clients and the kinds of food that they can offer. They asked for my students' help to determine how best to utilize the new space in a mission-aligned way.

Four groups of students tackled various elements of the project. One group researched national models for culinary arts training programs for homeless clients and, based on their findings, wrote a feasibility report for the Bridge House Board of Directors. Another group researched food sourcing and food-recovery models in Boulder. They contacted over 30 organic farms in the area to determine how they distribute produce and whether they would work with Bridge House to offer donations and skills classes for gardening, preserving, and preparing food. They wrote up their findings in a research report that they delivered to the Bridge House board members. A third group created and wrote all material for a website on which they gathered seasonal recipes of healthy meals that source local ingredients and worked on a plan for the Bridge House to better utilize its community garden space. The website, http://bridgehouserecipes.blogspot.com, is accessible to Bridge House clients at the commercial kitchen. Because the Bridge House clients said that they wanted to use the kitchen to provide food for other hungry populations in Boulder County, a fourth group of students researched national models and local competitors and devised a business plan for producing and marketing organic soup, which sources local ingredients, to generate revenue to feed food insecure people. They named their product Sustainabowl Soups. All student groups presented their research and recommendations to the Bridge House Board of Directors and staff during the final class of the semester.

As a class, students helped to educate Bridge House staff about the benefits of locally sourced and produced goods and to facilitate discussion between the Bridge House and local producers, businesses, and non-profit organizations dedicated to food re-localization. In this way, students embedded themselves within a grassroots re-localization and food justice initiative that moved far beyond the typical "server/served" model of traditional soup kitchens to a multi-dimensional model where Bridge House clients actively participate in feeding themselves and other members of the community, receive job training, become food literate, and generate revenue in the process.

When students read about and research food issues, they inevitably consider their own food purchasing and access options. To help facilitate a discussion on the University of Colorado campus about the kinds of food available to students, a group of writing students in another food-themed course set out to work with University of Colorado Dining Services, which had recently hired a Sustainability Coordinator and wanted to increase its purchase of local food. My students drafted a survey, which they distributed to University of Colorado students in front of several dining halls, to determine how the university will define "local food." The survey and the students' written report became a means toward discussion and education on campus. One of several definitional questions that students came up with concerned Rudi's Bread, a local bread company that uses ingredients shipped from around the country. Should Dining Services count Rudi's in their goal of purchasing 10% local food, students asked? Flour sourced from a ConAgra plant in Denver? Tuna canned in a Denver plant? As they delved into the environmental, economic, and cultural complexities of the issue, the students experienced living examples of multifaceted definitional arguments in working with Dining Services, the hundreds of students they surveyed, and local-food non-profits to create a working definition that the University could adopt.

While each of these examples of class projects illustrates students doing "critical" campus and community-based food literacy work that ties to food sovereignty and food justice, the projects evolved out of the critical thinking and problem-solving work that they did before the projects began and without which the projects would not have happened. Students listened to the community partners' constituents about what they already knew, what they needed to learn, and what they envisioned. They learned to adapt their arguments to the various audiences to which they presented their information in a variety of genres. Students gained valuable problem-solving skills as they delved into the complexities of the situation and made choices to ensure the sustainability of their projects. In other words, the movement toward social justice happened as a direct result of critical thinking standards deliberately integrated into course discussions and assignments. The depth and nuance of analysis and argument that we hope to see in student writing can grow out of the carefully planned service-learning course that deliberately maps experience and assignments to learning goals and that moves students to gradually answer the "What?", "So what?", and "Now what?" questions[7].

In higher-education institutions across the country, faculty and administrators argue that service-learning and community-engaged work be supported, funded, and included in reappointment, promotion, and tenure considerations. When practitioners tie rhetoric and composition learning objectives to community initiatives that promote social justice, students' community-based work can offer powerful, active-learning experiences. Clearly articulating the intended *academic* purposes of that critical service-learning work helps practitioners and administrators to achieve greater precision in "generating, deepening, and documenting" desired rhetoric and composition learning goals (Ash and Clayton 27). Assessment in composition studies shows that students learn to be more effective writers when writing in context for particular audiences. More specifically, studies on the impacts of service-learning in composition classes indicate that service-learning composition students demonstrate higher levels of rhetorical awareness, understanding of counterarguments, understanding of how to tailor language to particular contexts, and understanding of the complexity of arguments than do students in traditional composition courses (Bacon; Wurr; Feldman)[8].

That is the argument we need to make, and that is an argument my dean would support.

Endnotes

1. See 2013 CCCCs pre-conference workshop description "The Political Turn: Writing Democracy For the 21st Century" for discussion of the origin and development of this "political turn" movement, introduced by Deborah Mutnick, Steve Parks, and Shannon Carter. Their premise, articulated in the workshop description, is that "In this moment of mounting, worldwide economic, environmental, and cultural uncertainty, we submit that it is time for a 'political turn.'"

2. Adler-Kassner defines frames as the "organizing principles that are socially shared and persistent over time, that work symbolically to meaningfully structure the social world" (Reese 11, quoted in Adler-Kassner 37).

3. The food movement is but one of many social issues that one could address in service-learning classes. I offer my work with it as a model, but the theoretical ideas that this article presents could be applied to a host of topics.

4. I'm distinguishing here between what I would call genre-based service-learning courses such as grant writing or digital storytelling, where the objective is that students learn to produce a product in a particular genre for the non-profit partner, and theme-based courses, which more naturally lend themselves to the kind of reflective practice that moves students toward thinking about social justice issues.

5. I would like to thank my University of Colorado Boulder colleague, Elaina Verveer, for providing the tree image.

6. Ash and Clayton create three categories of learning, which they call "personal growth," "civic leaning," and "academic enhancement" (29).

7. While I do not believe that all service-learning courses without the social justice component are poorly constructed or have lower outcomes, I do believe that we cannot claim that we want certain kinds of learning without deliberately teaching for those learning goals.

8. Bringle, Hatcher, and Muthiah's large-scale longitudinal study indicates that service-learning students respond positively to the pedagogy that enhances their learning. These students show higher retention and graduation rates, and students with volunteer experiences, not limited to service-learning, donate to their alma mater at higher levels.

Works Cited

Adler-Kassner, Linda. *The Activist WPA: Changing Stories About Writing and Writers.* Logan, UT: Utah State University Press, 2008. Print.

Ash, Sarah L., Patti Clayton, and Maxine Atkinson. "Integrating Reflection and Assessment to Capture and Improve Student Learning." *Michigan Journal of Community Service Learning*, 11(2) 2005: 49-60. Web.

Ash, Sarah L. and Patti H. Clayton. "Generating, Deepening, and Documenting Learning: The Power of Critical Reflection in Applied Learning." *Journal of Applied Learning in Higher Education* 1(Fall), 25-48, 2009. Web.

Astin, A. W. and Sax, L. J. "How Undergraduates are Affected by Service Participation." *Journal of College Student Development*, 39, 1998: 251-263. Print.

Bacon, Nora. "The Trouble with Transfer: Lessons from a Study of Community Service Writing." *Michigan Journal of Community Service Learning* 6.1, 53-62, 1999. Print.

Bartlett, Al. "Arithmetic, Population, and Energy: A Talk by Al Bartlett." Web. 29 Mar. 2013. <http://www.albartlett.org/presentations/arithmetic_population_energy_video1.html>.

Berlin, James. *Rhetorics, Poetics, and Cultures.* Urbana, IL: NCTE, 1996. Print.

Bizzell, Patricia. "Composition Studies Saves the World!" *College English* 72.2 (2009): 174-187. Print.

Bringle, Robert G. and Julie A. Hatcher. "Reflection in Service-Learning: Making Meaning of Experience." *Educational Horizons* 77 (1999): 179-185. Print.

Bringle, Robert G., Julie A. Hatcher, and Richard N. Muthiah. "The Role of Service-Learning in the Retention of First-Year Students to Second Year." *Michigan Journal of Community Service Learning.* Spring 2010: 38-49. Print.

Brownlee, Michael. "The Local Food and Farming Revolution." *Transition Times. Transition Times*, 18 Mar. 2013. Web. < http://transition-times.com/blog/2010/03/08/the-local-food-and-farming-revolution/>.

Cipolle, Susan Benigni. *Service-Learning and Social Justice: Engaging Students in Social Change.* Lanham, MD: Rowman & Littlefield, Inc. 2010. Print.

Deans, Thomas. *Writing Partnerships: Service-Learning in Composition.* Urbana, IL: National Council of Teachers of English, 2000. Print.

Durst, Russel K.. *Collision Course: Conflict, Negotiation, and Learning in College Composition.* Urbana, IL: National Council of Teachers of English, 1999. Print.

Ellsworth, Elizabeth. "Why Doesn't This Feel Empowering?" *Harvard Educational Review* 59.3 (1989): 297-325. Web.

Eyler, Janet and Dwight E. Giles, Jr. *Where's the Learning in Service-Learning?* San Francisco: Jossey-Bass, 1999. Print.

Eyler, Janet, Dwight E. Giles, Jr., Stenson, C. M., & Gray, C. J. *At a Glance: What We Know About the Effects of Service-Learning on College Students, Faculty, Institutions and Communities, 1993-2000.* 3rd ed. Nashville, TN: Vanderbilt University Press, 2001. Print.

Family Learning Center. Web. 12 Ap. 2013. <http://www.flcboulder.org>.

Feigenbaum, Paul. "Traps, Tricksters, and the Long Haul: Negotiating the Progressive Teacher's Challenge in Literacy Education." *Reflections* 11.2 (2012): 5-38. Print.

Feldman, Anne. Making Writing Matter. Albany, NY: SUNY Press, 2008. Print.

Fish, Stanley. "What Should Colleges Teach?" *New York Times. New York Times*, August 24, 2009. Web. 13 Ap. 2013. <http://opinionator.blogs.nytimes.com/2009/08/24/what-should-colleges-teach/>.

———. *Save the World on Your Own Time*. New York: Oxford UP, 2008. Print.

Freire, Paulo. *Pedagogy of the Oppressed*. Trans. Myra Bergman Ramos. New York: Seabury, 1970. Print.

Gale, Xin Liu. *Teachers, Discourses, and Authority in the Postmodern Composition Classroom*. Albany, NY: SUNY Press, 1996. Print.

Gallagher, Chris. *Radical Departures: Composition and Progressive Pedagogy*. Urbana, IL: NCTE, 2002. Print.

Giroux, Henry. *Schooling and the Struggle for Public Life: Critical Pedagogy in the Modern Age*. Minneapolis: U of Minnesota P, 1988. Print.

Giroux, Henri. "A Critical Interview With Henri Giroux." *Global Education Magazine*. Creative Common, 30 Jan. 2013. Web. 2 Feb. 2013. <http://www.globaleducationmagazine.com/critical-interview-henry-giroux/>.

Harris, Joseph, "Revision As a Critical Practice" College English 65.6 (2003): 577-592. Print.

House, Veronica. "The Reflective Course Model: Changing the Rules for Reflection in Service-Learning Composition Courses" *Reflections: Journal of Public Rhetoric, Civic Writing, and Service-Learning*. 12.2 (2013): 27-65. Print.

Lynch, Paul. "Composition as a Thermostatic Activity." *College Composition and Communication* 60.4 (2009): 728-45. Print.

Mathieu, Paula. *Tactics of Hope: The Public Turn in English Composition*. Portsmouth, NH: Boynton/Cook Publishers, 2005. Print.

McIntosh, W.A. "Writing the Food Studies Movement: A Response." 3 June 2010. Web. 21 Ap. 2011. <http://www.foodpolitics.com/wp-content/uploads/02-FCS13.2-Nestle.pdf>

Mitchell, Tania D.. "Traditional vs. Critical Service-Learning: Engaging the Literature to Differentiate Two Models." *Michigan Journal of Community Service Learning* Spring 2008: 50-65. Print.

Nestle, Marion. "Writing the Food Studies Movement." 3 June 2010. Web. 21 Ap. 2011.<http://www.foodpolitics.com/wp-content/uploads/02-FCS13.2-Nestle.pdf>

Owens, Derek. *Composition and Sustainability: Teaching for a Threatened Generation*. Urbana, IL: NCTE, 2001. Print.

Parks, Stephen. *Gravyland: Writing Beyond the Curriculum in the City of Brotherly Love*. Syracuse, NY: Syracuse University Press, 2010. Print.

Seitz, David. "Hard Lessons Learned Since the First Generation of Critical Pedagogy." *College English* 64.4(2000): 503-12. Print.

Shor, Ira. *When Students Have Power.* Chicago, IL: University of Chicago Press, 1996. Print.

Wurr, Adrian. "Text-Based Measures of Service-Learning Writing Quality." *Reflections* 2.2 (2002): 40-55. Print.

Yoon, K. Hyoejin. "Affecting the Transformative Intellectual: Questioning "Noble" Sentiments in Critical Pedagogy and Composition." *JAC* 25.4 , 2005 pp.717-759. Print.

Author Bio

Dr. Veronica House is Associate Faculty Director for Service-Learning and Outreach in the Program for Writing and Rhetoric at the University of Colorado Boulder. As founder of the University's Writing Initiative for Service and Engagement (WISE), she created the first service-learning Writing and Rhetoric courses for first-year students and has coordinated the Program for Writing and Rhetoric's transformation into one of the only writing programs in the country to have integrated service-learning throughout its lower- and upper-division curriculum. For this work, she was awarded the University's *Women Who Make a Difference Award in 2009* and the writing program's *Award for Excellence and Innovation in Teaching* in 2013. She works with faculty at colleges and universities across the country to design community-engaged learning courses and "engaged" departments and serves on Campus Compact of the Mountain West's Advisory Committee.

Assembling for Agency: Prisoners and College Students in a Life Writing Workshop

David Coogan

Rhetorical theorists have argued that agency is a communal experience, but material conditions in jail *and* society often prevent prisoners and college students from experiencing it in meaningful ways that embrace difference. Challenging those conditions by bringing both groups together in a writing workshop enables everyone to resist discourses that would name them and to inquire, collaboratively, about pressing social problems like gun violence. This essay shows how a prisoner and a college student sustained that inquiry in writing, moving from *metanoia* or regret into *kairos*—the seizing of their day and the experience of agency. The ultimate value of that experience transcends the here and now of the workshop to become the building block of a better public sphere.

In his book about the end of Chicago's high-rise public housing, *City of Rhetoric: Revitalizing the Public Sphere in Metropolitan America*, David Fleming reveals an all-too-familiar disjuncture between Rhetoric's high ideals for democracy and its gritty translation into the real. It comes through the story of transforming one of these communities, Cabrini Green, into condos with shared public areas and a storytelling project for economically and racially diverse residents. Though the urban planners from the city did not characterize it this way, Fleming argues convincingly that a polis had been envisioned—a community that "literally sets aside time and space for the rendering and negotiation of conflicts"(13). Incredibly, the same public life that we theorize in our scholarship and commend to students in community literacy projects was at hand: not the shouting of pundits or the dead ends of polemics but the honorable efforts of ordinary people making claims, telling stories, presenting evidence, and presumably, compromising in service of something larger and nobler. Then Rhetoric became rhetoric again.

When the plan was made public, condo-buying "investors" were characterized in the press as the brave ones doing the right thing by integrating with the dangerous ones. Naturally, some from Cabrini resisted this characterization—their elbows in need of this middle-class rubbing—and came up with a counter plan: to buy their building from the city. This triggered a competition in public discourse between the rhetoric of *nobles oblige,* on the one hand, and *solidarity* amongst poor African Americans on the other, with impatient strains overheard in the background—a barely contained excitement to just blow up "the projects" already and all of the fears and loathing they had come to represent. Of course, the buildings came down to make way for the mixed-income community minus the ambitious storytelling project. And when they did, the "real winners," Fleming concludes, were the "white, child-less couples who scored cheap housing" (213) on prime city real estate while displaced residents got pushed farther and farther to the city borders, carrying with them only the Section 8 vouchers for apartments that most landlords were under no legal obligation to honor.

Though Fleming's study does not feature himself or his students going public to argue the case for saving these buildings from the wrecking balls, what he does feature is the common challenge facing teachers, writers, and scholars with like-minded visions of promoting justice with their rhetoric while having to contend with forces much more powerful than rhetoric. And in that sense, it is instructive. We know from research in political science, he explains, that "the highest levels of political activity" often take "place in the most economically diverse places, apparently, because the conflict stimulated by heterogeneity increases civic participation among residents" (48). Yet homogenous neighborhoods in cities or suburbs, with their "isolation" and "functional segregation," all but ensure there is "little to argue about" (48-9). A "fear of difference," it would seem, has been built right into the environment. And in the case of land-use politics in Chicago, that built-in fear simply stomped the rosy ideals of urban planning. Substitute "community literacy" or "service learning" for urban planning, and you can see where I'm headed. We may want our rhetoric to make a difference. But difference might not want—or even notice—our rhetoric.

If this were only a problem in Chicago or even a problem specific to cities, Fleming's trouble might well be his own—a sentimental streak about urban planning, perhaps, or the familiar pining for the polis in rhetorical theory. But the underlying challenge of making a polis filled with diverse stakeholders capable of sustaining critical dialogue about problems that affect the common good is not unique to cities or urban planning. It's a challenge of reaching beyond our familiar "communities of the like-minded" (Fleming 14), a challenge that is as much practical as it is rhetorical.

For me, there is no greater reminder of that reaching then when I am walking single file in silence with my college students, the only baker's dozen of both genders in street clothes, flush up against the wall in the hall of the Richmond City Jail, behind the yellow line, waiting for our guide to open a steel door; waiting again for prisoners in jump suits to clear an area before we get the cue to walk again, stop again. When we walk to this class that only meets at the jail, we realize we are far from our familiar community of like-minded students and professors who, if they share nothing else, share the freedom of wearing whatever they like and walking wherever they choose, unescorted and unguided by a yellow line. In this long hallway there is no fitting in. But once we enter the classroom we call our sanctuary and our incarcerated classmates, a few minutes later, join us, it becomes possible to find a meaningful, if momentary, fit.

Like the ancients who assembled in forums to enter into a realm of freedom with their words, we assemble here to persuade and to be persuaded, to identify and to question identifications, to open ourselves to the possibility of change in jail and in society. This is a hopeful practice, a ritual, even—coming together to write and share what we have read. We write in search of freedom together. Yet we write with full awareness that even this freedom to write could be taken from us—that our assembly is a temporary privilege for pursuing common ground across the many boundaries that seem to divide us: e.g., race, class, gender, age, experiences with violence, drugs, crime, incarceration. Our assembly cannot change the facts of these divisions. Yet assembling does defy the determinism of existing material conditions in the jail and in our city by creating opportunities for everyone to resist discursive practices and group identities emanating from those conditions; making public collective concerns and regrets; dwelling in a collective *metanoia* of our lives; and discovering *kairos*—to seize the time in writing and sharing. Assembling for a life-writing workshop is not just a hopeful practice, then, but a rhetorical one that promotes the experience of agency and the exercise of citizenship as active, collaborative phenomena—words and deeds that would not occur outside assembly.

My collaborator and friend, john Dooley, a poet and GED teacher with over thirty years of experience at the jail, and the person making this writing workshop—this assembly—possible, puts it better:

> The very process of writing and sharing as we do in our classes invites us, sometimes as a soft song, sometimes as a siren, sometimes as a rip – current, to draw nearer and nearer to the rivers of inspiration that give expression to those near, near me. Our writings and our sharings give expression to all that we are. Our expressions reach far down in to our darkest moments and places, whisper like the sea our mysterious languages of our unique truths, and, with our sacred permissions, reveal our tenderness and joys and our consciousness and our aloneness and the very underlying opposites which permeate our very existence. Through our writings and sharings, through compassionate listenings, we are able to integrate each other's sorrows and joys and horrors and humor and contradictions. Thereby, with written and spoken permissions, we are able to enter vast, deep, personal spiritual passageways to the very essence of who we are and how we feel and how we see the world. Our writings and our sharings are our sanctuaries, places wherein and wherefrom we may remember who we are as human beings, living souls.

I do appreciate having a poet—*this* poet—lead my students and me to class. It helps that he's huge, tall, and tattooed, speaks in a low baritone, jokes, and gets enormous respect from the men he brings to school and has no problem, none whatsoever, kicking them out of school for breaking his rules, which amount to common sense and decency: no negativity, no slacking, no "N" word or denigrating talk about women— just cheerful study, honest and open. All of that helps, but what really helps is that he understands that a diverse group like ours writing about our lives will stumble into "the very underlying opposites which permeate our very existence." The right response is patience and humility, to try holding those opposites in our hands without breaking them, integrating each other's "sorrows and joys and horrors and humor and contradictions." When we do it is because we have tapped into what Carolyn Miller calls the "kinetic energy of rhetorical performance":

> The Greek root of energy is ergon, deed or work, and energeia is the deed in the doing, action itself. If agency is a potential energy, it will be thought of as a possession or property of an agent (like a stationary stone), but if agency is a kinetic energy, it must be a property of the rhetorical event or performance itself. (147)

Of course, kinetic energy does not just circulate because we convene a class. Just the same we should not underestimate the difficulty of convening a class and its protean power. As Karlyn Campbell reminds us, agency is "communal, social, cooperative, and participatory and, simultaneously, constituted and constrained by the material and symbolic elements of context and culture" (3).

There's only so much agency prisoners at this jail, the Richmond City Jail, can constitute when they are constrained on their open and overcrowded tiers by the "context and culture" of fellow prisoners talking crime, running games on each other, or in other ways spinning their wheels with nothing to do and too many people to do it with. Just the same, there's only so much agency college students can constitute when they are constrained by the "material and symbolic" borders of our urban campus, where talk about crime and prison can either be concrete—the student who got robbed last month—or abstract—a pendulum of political positions, a constellation of pop culture references. It may seem strange to say it like this, but prisoners and free citizens need each other to cultivate agency in ways that resist their shared restriction within these "material and symbolic" boundaries. What they need is that opportunity to find in each other the agency they crave. Yet "if agency is an attribution," writes Miller:

> Our ideological concerns have been misplaced. We should be concerned less about empowering subaltern subjects and more about enabling and encouraging attributions of agency to them by those with whom they interact—and accepting such attributions from them. We should examine the attributions we ourselves are willing to make and work to improve the attributions that (other) empowered groups are willing to make. (153)

That is what it means to cultivate agency: to consider which attributions we are "willing to make" and willing to help others make. It is not the case, in other words, that college students, by virtue of their status as students, their literacy, and so on, are the ones "giving" agency to the less empowered and less literate, but that both work to find moments in which they can attribute agency to the other—to interrupt what Patricia Roberts-Miller characterizes as the "security" of ingroup/outgroup thinking (180) and the "naïve realism" and "essentialism" it requires—an essentialism we are more likely to hold close when we are secure in the communities we know best. Assembling across difference to experience a new kind of agency is enormously useful and sadly unusual for people who more often experience rhetoric in the community or even in college as the *reinforcement* of preconceived ideas and *affirmation* of group identities.

To illustrate these claims, I offer a rhetorical analysis of two students' attempts to resist group identities as "violent" or as the "victim of violence"—two students whose writings together carve out a more complicated alternative to those characterizations and storylines in public discourse. Their writings emerged from a service-learning course, Writing and Social Change, which has the following objectives:

• To evaluate your life experiences and values, writing out a vision of where you've been and where you're going in life in response to a range of readings in poetry, fiction and non-fiction

• To share those writings with your classmates in spirit of mutual respect and inquiry, developing a theme out of that inquiry and conducting research to answer your questions whenever necessary

• To revise your writing—refine your inquiry—based, in part, on the feedback you get

• To create a portfolio of polished pieces or one single piece—20 pages of it, typed, double-spaced

• To articulate a theme or a set of themes running throughout that body of work in a cover letter (Coogan 1)

What I am looking at now are the final portfolios of Isreal and Jesse: 25 to 30 pages of poems, essays, flash autobiographies, and reflections drafted in class in response to prompts and revised out of class. The prompts asked them to write about a place they know well and to write about a time they experienced violence in some way (as perpetrator, victim, by-stander, etc.). Some of these writings also appeared in our class anthology, which was made public to the Sheriff's staff and guests from VCU at a reading. Even so, I asked each man if I could quote from his portfolio in this essay, and each agreed. Both also signed release forms with the Sheriff's office and with VCU, giving us formal permission to make their work public.

As you can see from the first course objective, a large part of what we do is write to evaluate our histories so that we can better determine our futures. In my course description, I elaborate on the task as a "communal writing practice" where we:

> bear witness to the problems we see in our lives and in life. We will share our diverse experiences and together envision a world we can share that is more humane, more accommodating, more generous and sane; a world where there is less derailing, less crime and less pain. To do this, we will need to wrestle with the paradox at the heart of writing and social change; the burden of becoming a writer—becoming honest, creative and responsible with words and, presumably, the corresponding deeds—while struggling with the forces in jail and "out there" in society that would subvert our courageous choices. (Coogan 1)

In this way, the workshop asks writers to stare directly into their own choices in order to open themselves to a range of emotions, including regret. In a recent essay about metanoia, the neglected underbelly of kairos—the opportune moment—Kelly Myers has shown that this plumbing of the depths of regret or guilt can be considered a form of rhetorical invention. In ancient art, Kairos is the athletic one shown running, hair flying, triumphant. He's just made the right argument at the right time. Metanoia sits in the background with her melancholy. She's lost the chance to speak up. The implication is that unless you like being sad, you don't want to end up like Metanoia. Yet if we see metanoia as a necessary opportunity to reflect on a lost opportunity, it can be transformative. Metanoia enables the rhetor to synthesize the emotional, rational, and even spiritual dimensions of an experience that can lead him or her back to kairos and the exhilarating experience of agency.

Meyers goes on to note that in ancient texts about metanoia and kairos, there is often a "trusted teacher" enabling this growth. The lifewriting theorists, Sidonie Smith and Julia Watson, describe a similar role of "coaxer"—someone who helps another tell their story (68). What I want to argue for below, then, is the *social* experience of metanoia, the seizing of *our* day and days to come. By resisting the material conditions that make some stories, some storytellers, unknowable we are insisting that those stories and storytellers matter. Sharing these stories is not only valuable during the here and now of our workshop but in the larger work of the public sphere that we will take up as citizens after the workshop ends. We are building the kind of public sphere that we hope we will have an opportunity to build again.

The first hint we get that we will enter into a state of metanoia in Isreal's poem is the title, "If I Had My Life to Live over Again." While growing up, he explains, "I learned lessons through strangers, family and peers. Some were better and others for the worse. It is up to me to separate the gift from the curse." Before he even tells us the story we are made aware that if mistakes get made, he is to blame.

> I am isolating one moment which I can clearly see, with someone's life on the line. I am talking about me. A couple of big bags of smoke got me in a bind. He was still arguing when bullets started flying. No one was hit and I thought it was over. No need I thought to be looking over my shoulder.

But of course there was. "Time past," and the guy came back to shoot him in the leg: "I find myself facedown burning out of control. Is that shock or did my body separate from my soul? I'm being pulled but I feel no pain and I'm thinking 'If only I had my life to live over again.'" Bleeding in the street and wondering about his soul, however, quickly gives way to wanting revenge: "Just that fast I go from wanting to do better in life to thinking the worse. I want that pussy motherfucka in a hearse." After he heals and gets out of the hospital, he gets his chance:

> I race to the scene and pour out fire. Burned up his face like rubber off a tire. Put him in a trunk and took off across the water, saw my car on the news—shit

is really out of order. So I dump his ass and slide, go and hide my ride. Police all through the hood this shit ain't good. After a few weeks they get a tip and bring me in. Long story short I'm found guilty and sent to the pen. Left with the thought 'If I only had my life to live over again.'

Though the poem is mostly plotting a street drama, I'm struck by the swinging from regret to revenge—going "from wanting to do better to thinking the worse" and then, finally, wishing he could have "life to live over again." The problem is that we don't know what he regrets. Does he regret taking revenge because he almost killed someone or almost died? Because he shot at someone or got shot? We don't know and possibly he doesn't, at least not in this poem.

Jesse's first piece ends in much the same incomplete way. He poses the emotional problem that violence has created in his life while he struggles to resolve it. The story begins when he explains what happened when he "fell asleep watching television" at his house in another neighborhood closer to campus, a working-class area called Parkwood:

I woke up in what seemed like a dream to five or six handgun shots on the street outside my house. For a few seconds I floundered between the couch and the carpet. About the time I got to my feet I heard a car crash where the gun shots had come from. I didn't really think it through before I ran outside.

While he is memorizing the plates, he hears more shots and runs back inside to warn his brother and call the police. A flurry of miscommunication between him and the dispatcher and the officer on the scene, however, leads Jesse to conclude: "Whoever shot up my neighborhood and crashed into my neighbor's truck got out and away without much trouble." This in turn leads him to wonder about the trouble he had put himself into "trying to get the license plates" and "being a good neighbor." There is a cost—a new burden to carry now—and in some ways he regrets it.

I bought a police-style telescoping baton soon after and started carrying it all the time. I guess I just balanced my distrust with a bit of protection and I feel better. The feeling, the "better feeling, is not a satisfying one. I walk around standing taller, glancing over my shoulder with authority. It's exhausting to be so concerned and aware of safety all the time. It will be a welcome change to walk confidently and happily without the aid of a solid steel bludgeon or a gun.

I find it disconcerting—this image of Jesse exhausted "standing taller, glancing over" his shoulder. I am equally disconcerted by the image of Isreal "pouring out fire" on a rival and stuffing him in the trunk of his car to settle a beef about "a couple of big bags of smoke." It's more than disconcerting, actually. My emotional range starts somewhere in fear, sinks into despair, and then plummets towards disgust. But neither guy lets me keep these moods. "I chose my house," Jesse writes in his next piece, and "to an extent my neighborhood, to an even broader extent my neighbors." But these were

> Naïve choices. How blinded and/or ignorant must a person be in order for a choice to no longer be a choice? How naïve can a choice be and still be a choice? I visited my neighborhood a few times before homeownership. There were no shoot-outs, my car was not stolen during my investigative moments. This seems good, I see no reason why I shouldn't buy into this.

He clearly sees in retrospect that he had no basis for truly judging the neighborhood safe or unsafe and wonders aloud how much control any of us have over such choices. That second question, especially, seems wise—he wants to know just when choice becomes an illusion. But instead of dwelling further in his own regret, he extends himself into the minds of his classmates at the jail:

> Inmate X was raised with expectation and desire for unrealistic and unnecessary things. Inmate X without his acknowledgement, was corralled into prison prerequisites. Inmate X was not warned by trusted individuals, he was taught by his friends and parents. Inmate X tested the waters and found them pleasantly luke-warm. Inmate X chose to steal from a person who had more than enough. Inmate X chose to sell drugs that were sold to him for the first time only hours previous. Inmate X chose his cell next to his neighboring inmates who chose their cells and chose their jails. Who understands their choices? Who knows their options? Hindsight is still far from 20/20.

I am compelled by Jesse's reasoning here and his empathy about the process of social conditioning. Yet I am compelled, as well, by Isreal's counterargument. In his next piece, "Life as a Falcon," Isreal circles around Jesse's paradox—what I'll call the choice of no choice: "Girls or beefs, school or the streets, hustling or study hall, these shouldn't be hard decisions to make at all." Yet they were.

> The choices I made are obvious to me. I've lost myself out in the streets. Hustling, clowning, trying to be down. I've put more than few of my good friends in the ground. Now I'm in search for a piece of mind and I can't find it. Can't seem to get out of this fog from so many days of getting blinded. But that was my choice. I lost my DAMN MIND!

Why did he choose that life in the streets? In "The Turn Around," he explains that it was more or less a continuation of his earliest memories. As a little kid, he learned early on how to manipulate his mother, hustle the other kids out of their candy, talk his way out of beatings from his father, impress the older thuggish boys in the neighborhood, and organize kids to steal. This piece is written differently, too—with less swagger and rhyme. As he gropes for understanding, he compares his life to the Biblical character,

Israel. Though he spells his name differently from that character, Isreal sees himself like Israel, who was once known as Jacob before God called him to lead his people and form the nation of Israel. Before becoming Israel, Jacob was known as the deceiver or supplanter who fought his brother Esau in the womb and later tricked him out of his birthright with their dying father. In "The Turn Around," Isreal recounts his own early days as a young manipulator, thief, and drug dealer in the neighborhood, concluding:

> That was the Jacob in me while I was wrestling with God. Now I am on a newer path after God has touched my hip and made it hard for me to walk down that old path anymore. I'm grateful to have Him spare me and allow me to walk with Him. It could have been worse and I probably should be dead.

But when he tries following up on this "newer path" in his next piece, "Some Things Never Change," we are forced to acknowledge another paradox: trying to change in an environment that rewards you for not changing. This could very well be jail, but this piece is actually set in an imagined future after he is released from jail. In the piece, he reports on a conversation he had with an old associate about a program he has created for at-risk kids. His antagonist in the poem only knows Isreal by his Jacob-like street name, Fresh.

> *Seriously Fres—I mean Isreal you know I get money but I'm just coming home.*
>
> If you really are serious, I can put you on without putting your life on the line.
>
> *You mean you're gonna put me in charge of some heavy shit? I'm gone shine out this BITCH!*
>
> Cuz you are not paying attention at all and what you're talking about ain't gone happen dawg.
>
> *Yeah right, coke or dope—what's the name of the game?*
>
> I'm working hard with the kids in this program I started, trying to provide them with a better chance at success.
>
> *You cold blooded boy. You got kids pumping that shit too?*
>
> Dawg what the fuck is wrong with you? Do you hear what's coming out of my mouth?

The antagonist continues to not get it. And when he sort of gets it at the end, he quickly dismisses it because what Isreal is asking him to do as a mentor for young people sounds too much "like work." What this guy wants is "the party with the good weed and bad broads." Isreal sighs and shakes his head, realizing he can't help this guy "live another way" and concluding that "some things never change." Remarkably, Jesse confronts the same double bind in his last piece. In "Over the course of the semester," he writes:

> I have thought multiple times about the men in the jail classroom while I walk through my neighborhood watching my back. I'm not thinking about

those men in fear. I'm thinking about them in perplexity. I have befriended the men in the jail classroom. If I saw them today, whether on the street or in the jail, I would greet them warmly. I have yet to meet the men who live in my neighborhood and watch me greedily as I walk alone at night. I have heard their threats. I've responded by carrying a weapon. I can't help wondering: if we were in a writing group, think we could be friends? I know not every man is the same. I know that it takes a special person to accomplish what the men in the jail classroom have accomplished. I struggle with the fact that it took the attention of john, Dr. Coogan, and my other VCU students to set the process in action. I struggle only because the men in my neighborhood will not receive that sort of attention until they get locked up, maybe not even then.

What Jesse and Isreal both achieve here is that transformation of metanoia into kairos—reflection into action. Isreal's struggle to persuade his antagonist to join him as a community leader parallels Jesse's struggle to speak up to his menacing neighbors. Both identify the core challenge they'll face in the days to come. And both resist the lure of hero and victim stories, as Loraine Higgins and Lisa Brush characterize it in their study of welfare women writing: those ready-made narratives circulating all too easily, in this case, of having once been a victim of a violent environment and now becoming the hero who has easily, unambiguously risen above it as a persuasive community leader (Isreal) or an armed citizen protecting his turf (Jesse). Both know they are neither the heroes nor the victims of their stories but somewhere in between. They know what it is they don't know—an important disposition—as Myers elaborates, because it keeps the process of inquiry going:

> When people identify the roots of 'passionate commitments'—specific moments of conversion to belief, both their own and those of others—they create improved hope for more productive conversation. Therefore, kairos and metanoia can come into argument not only as an end goal (e.g., transforming another's opinion) but as an important part of the process that shifts conversation away from antagonism and toward dialogue. (16)

Though they remain ambivalent—unsure, unsatisfied—they remain open to dialogue, oriented toward change, and eager to build a more peaceful public life.

We have reason to be hopeful about the long-term impact of engaging one another as citizens in diverse public spheres like the one described here, especially because of the ever-evolving nature of public spheres. As Robert Asen notes:

> The value of greater participation lies not in its quantitative but its qualitative contributions. More voices bolster public agendas because they raise distinct perspectives and encourage different ways of participating. New nodes link up with existing nodes to create new pathways in the networks of the

public sphere. Engagement occurs amid points in existing networks, which themselves are always incomplete. (199)

None of us knows which networks we will find ourselves in the future. What is certain is that these networks need tending. Robert Waxler, a professor of English and the founder of Changing Lives through Literature, an alternative sentencing program, explains:

> We can best judge the vitality of a democratic community, we believe, by how inclusive it is—not by how many voices it has excluded but by how many are engaged, not by how many people are incarcerated but by how many can speak out as citizens. [That's why he] suggested to a local judge concerned with 'turnstile justice' (as he characterized the problem then) that offenders who are sent behind bars from his bench, eventually released, then returned before his bench again might fare better by reading literature and talking about it around a table on a college campus. And so might the rest of the community as well. (679)

What Waxler intended when he formed the program was not simply to stop turnstile justice but to revitalize democracy and engage community. And the obstacles to community are everywhere. Isreal's antagonist in that last piece, the one who keeps calling him his street name, clearly lacks that incentive to engage a new community. So do the ones loitering on the street near Jesse's home. Isreal and Jesse, however, have found it—they had their chance to assemble and write and share what would otherwise go unwritten and unconsidered. They were cultivated to become better citizens with the rhetorical arts. As Kurt Spellmeyer describes it:

> The relevance of the arts, Adorno suggests, lies in their promising of 'what is not real' (122), and this openness sets the stage for an experimental 'heterogeneity' tolerated less and less everywhere today except in the humanities, where it is actually prized (132). Precisely because of this ability to occupy the liminal space between reality and representation, the arts and the allied humanities—English in particular—are the social sites best positioned to preserve the diversity now under siege. (575)

When we assemble in the name of "experimental heterogeneity," we are searching collaboratively for "what is not real" within the discursive hegemony constraining us. Or as Roberts-Miller might argue, when we assemble to challenge group identities, we are cultivating critical thinking about the links we make, at times, imperceptibly between what we see in our built environment—and from this evidence what we would claim to be true—and what we might believe about ourselves, others, and the real—based on what we imagine should be real. When Jesse returns home, he literally sees the people on the street differently just as Isreal, returning to the streets in his mind, imagines an encounter with an associate differently. Both resist the lure of their old group identities: criminal leader and fearful homeowner. This is a small but significant first step toward steering public discourse in the right direction or, as Jenny Edbauer might characterize it, a positive first step toward generating a new and more inclusive rhetorical ecology.

These links that I have been making between assembly, agency, writing, and citizenship in an ever-changing public sphere may challenge some weary of overreaching. Amy Wan, for example, has conceded that most "scholars use citizenship and its rhetorical cachet as a way to imagine students as agents beyond the institution," as I am doing here, but that the problem with this is that

> these invocations are premised upon unspoken, casual, or ambient assumptions about citizenship itself: the belief that one only needs to act as a citizen through participation in a community or society in order to become a citizen, or the resulting wholesale acceptance of citizenship as a meaningful product of effective writing instruction. This is not sufficient. (33)

Wan's concern is that our casual or "aspirational" linking between citizenship and writing begs too many questions. Looking out from the classroom into society makes her wonder how exactly learning to write makes you a better citizen. Writing teachers who claim that they are doing citizenship by teaching writing should probably think more critically about the habits they are instilling in students that, in the teachers' minds, will lead them to become better citizens beyond their classrooms. The problem I see is not in the warning but in the assumption that citizenship is best learned from a classroom on campus.

So much more can be seen and so much more can be gained from classrooms that assemble college students and citizen-writers in the community in ways that confront the "fear of difference" that Fleming has articulated—the challenge to make attributions of agency to each other as they search, collaboratively, for a better public life together. What happens as a result of those attributions, of course, is uncertain and not entirely ours to determine, as Paula Mathieu and Diana George remind us:

> Successful circulation of public writing is not achieved by going it alone, but through networks of relationships, in alliances between those in power and those without, through moments of serendipity. Any changes made or attempted can't be located solely on the page, or in the act of composition, but also are found in the writing's circulation, in how it works in the world, fostering conversation, creating pressure, and even creating unexpected allies. (144)

Our public work with students and community members may foster conversation, create pressure or unexpected allies, or it may not. Outcomes can be vexing. This why Nathaniel Rivers and Ryan Weber do not require their students in a first-year-writing class to go public with their proposed interventions into the rhetorical ecologies that interest them: they do not want to subject their students to the messy experience of trying to reach short-term outcomes in a semester or—perhaps the worst experience of all—failing to notice or even appropriately respond to those outcomes. Outcomes are not easily led by rhetoric. Fleming's study of Cabrini Green has proven that. But it has also proven a truism I can verify: what is easy to do is not necessarily worth doing.

I learned that during my first writing workshop at the jail in 2006 as a volunteer with a local nonprofit organization, Offender Aid and Restoration. Nothing was guaranteed. My time slot and classroom location, the chapel—one of three open spaces for gatherings like this—were easily taken from me like canteen by stronger, more powerful service providers, typically ministers. Men I came to know over many months of drafting and digging into the vulnerabilities of their lives would one day be gone—released, shipped to prison—without warning, much less a goodbye. Lockdowns because of fighting, airborne viruses, or no particularly good reason would stop all volunteer activities like mine indefinitely. Even when we had class, it could be interrupted by guards—students pulled—at any time. You would think jail would be the one place, the one classroom, without tardiness or unexcused absences, but students were late all the time or would sometimes fail to show due to court dates, visits, etc. Or they would be stranded on the tier without an escort to the chapel—punished for something they did—or did not do—the day before.

The disjuncture between education and incarceration is real, one that we sometimes manage to pass through but that we cannot pass off or pretend not to see or smooth over with our own heroic ideas of overcoming the barriers—passing notes, contraband, through razor wire, as Tobi Jacobi describes it. This disjuncture is widely known by educators working with prisoners. Buzz Alexander, the founder of Prison Creative Arts Program at the University of Michigan, describes his workshops with prisoners and college students as "chaotic, disrupted, difficult, contentious, marked by struggle, collaborative and in the end familial. What keeps it going is that we trust everyone to make it happen" (PMLA 551). What they trust is that they *can* and *should* help each other resolve the struggle for identity that writing opens up. Stephen Hartnett, another long-time prison teacher and communications scholar, adds that what you learn from the experience is that "by transforming the terror in your life into art and by then bravely sharing it, you learn to trust yourself and earn the respect of others" (PMLA 552). It is a rare opportunity in a place better known for squashing opportunity.

Even now, six years later, after having grown my volunteer writing workshop into Open Minds, a part of our curriculum in the English department, an interdisciplinary program in the humanities, and a source of continuing education units to incarcerated students—a program that has won grants and awards from my university and is praised by the Sheriff, I still experience what Alexander calls the chaotic struggle of assembly, and I still treasure it. Assembling may not change the larger realities and injustices of incarceration, but it matters a great deal to the ones assembling: prisoners; college students and their professors in Women's Studies and Religious Studies and African-American studies and English; and hundreds of people, incarcerated and free, who have taken these classes and will go on to inhabit the real spaces and the ideals of our shared public life, and whose words and actions mattered in class and will matter in the lives they will lead after class..

Sometimes when I'm telling someone about this work, the person will ask me if it scares me to go to the jail. My college students who join me in the sanctuary sometimes face the same wide eyes or even anger when they tell friends or family they're taking a class with "those people." It takes a while—and a willing listener—to convey the reality that the experience is humbling and inspiring. Other listeners, of course, already share that feeling—a heartfelt, head-nodding contentment that it's great sharing your story with prisoners sharing theirs. Both reactions are intense. I've never gotten blasé. And it's taken me years to see that these reactions come from the same nerve center. They show awareness that a door has been opened that everyone thought was shut. You can hear the sounds of prisoners now, their voices mingling with yours in public. And in that instant, you imagine what our world would be like—what public discourse would sound like—if we heard more of it, more of us. And you know right away how you feel about that.

Works Cited

Asen, Robert. "A Discourse of Citizenship." *Quarterly Journal of Speech* 90.2 (May 2004): 189-211. Print.

Campbell, Karlyn. Agency: Promiscuous and Protean. *Communication and Critical/ Cultural Studies* 2.1(March 2005): 1-19. Print.

Coogan, David. *Writing and Social Change Syllabus.* Fall 2012. Department of English, Virginia Commonwealth University, Richmond, VA. Microsoft Word file.

Edbauer, Jenny. "Unframing Models of Public Deliberation: From Rhetorical Situation to Rhetorical Ecologies." *Rhetoric Society Quarterly* 35.4 (Fall 2005): 5-24. Print.

Fleming, David. *City of Rhetoric: Revitalizing the Public Sphere in Metropolitan America.* New York: SUNY Press, 2008.

Flower, Linda. *Community Literacy and the Rhetoric of Public Engagement.* Carbondale: Southern Illinois University Press, 2008.

Higgins, Lorraine D. and Lisa Brush. "Personal Experience Narrative and Public Debate: Writing the Wrongs of Welfare." *College Composition and Communication* 57.4 (June 2006): 694-729. Print.

Jacobi, Tobi. "Slipping Pages through Razor Wire: Literacy Action Projects in Jail." *Community Literacy* 2.2 (2008). Print.

Mathieu, Paula and Diana George. "Not Going It Alone: Public Writing, Independent Media, and the Circulation of Homeless Advocacy." *College Composition and Communication* 61.1 (September 2009): 130-149. Print.

Miller, Carolyn. "What Can Automation Tell Us About Agency?" *Rhetoric Society Quarterly* 37.2 (Spring 2007): 137-157. Print.

Myers, Kelly A. "Metanoia and the Transformation of Opportunity." *Rhetoric Society Quarterly* 41.1: 1-18. Print.

PMLA Editor's Column. "Prisons, Activism, and the Academy—A Roundtable with Buzz Alexander, Bell Gale Chevigny, Stephen John Hartnett, Janie Paul and Judith Tannenbaum." *Publication of the Modern Language Association* 123.3 (May 2008): 545-567.

Rivers, Nathaniel and Ryan Weber. "Ecological, Pedagogical, Public Rhetoric." *College Composition and Communication* 63.2 (December 2011): 187-218. Print.

Roberts-Miller, Patricia. "Dissent as 'Aid and Comfort to the Enemy': The Rhetorical Power of Naïve Realism and Ingroup Identity." *Rhetoric Society Quarterly* 39.2 (April 2009): 170-188. Print.

Smith, Sidonie and Julia Watson. *Reading Autobiography: A Guide for Interpreting Life Narratives*. Minneapolis, MN: University of Minnesota Press, 2010.

Spellmeyer, Kurt. "Opinion: Saving the Social Imagination." *College English* 74.6 (July 2012): 567-585. Print.

Waxler, Robert. "Changing Lives Through Literature." *Publication of the Modern Language Association* 123.3 (May 2008): 678-683. Print.

Wan, Amy J. "In the Name of Citizenship: The Writing Classroom and the Promise of Citizenship." *College Composition and Communication* 74.1 (September 2011): 28-49. Print.

Author Bio

David Coogan is an associate professor of English, Director of Undergraduate Studies, and Co-Director of Open Minds, a Partnership between Virginia Commonwealth University and the Richmond City Sheriff's Office (www.openminds.vcu.edu). With John Ackerman, he co-authored *The Public Work of Rhetoric: Citizen Scholars and Civic Engagement* and numerous book chapters and essays about community literacy, writing, and social change.

"Socializing Democracy": The Community Literacy Pedagogy of Jane Addams

Rachael Wendler

> This article reclaims Jane Addams as a community literacy pedagogue and explicates her pedagogical theory through an analysis of her social thought. Addams' goal of "socializing democracy" through education led her to both encourage immigrant students to associate across difference and to assimilate into dominant literacies—tensions present in today's community literacy contexts. The article includes suggestions for rhetorically redeploying Addams' pedagogy in contemporary writing instruction.

> The educational activities of a Settlement, as well its philanthropic, civic, and social undertakings, are but differing manifestations of the attempt to socialize democracy, as is the very existence of the Settlement itself
> —Jane Addams, 1902

The closure of Jane Addams' Hull House in 2012 was a milestone in the history of community literacy. For over 120 years, the Hull House had provided literacy instruction, along with a wealth of other human services, to the diverse neighborhoods on the West Side of Chicago. Much has been written on Jane Addams' role in founding the American settlement house movement, influencing the philosophy of famed education scholar John Dewey, shaping modern social work theory, and catalyzing progressive-era social reforms (Peaden, Robbins, Deegan), yet Addams' significant historical role as a community literacy pedagogue has often gone unrecognized.

As a community-literacy forerunner in the early 1900s, Addams led the Hull House in hosting a wide range of innovative community-literacy activities, from literature and political theory reading clubs to place-based adult ESL classes, community theatre, and social-action writing groups. In her twelve books and over five hundred articles, Addams had quite a bit to say about teaching literacy in community contexts. Her writings, along with memoirs of Hull House clients and student texts, provide a portrait of a literacy worker who challenged existing ideas about educating underserved populations, invested in teaching language as a form of social action, and developed a broad notion of literacy that extended beyond functional literacy to include cultural, workplace, and political literacies.

In this article, I work to reconstruct Addams' community literacy pedagogy: first to reclaim Addams as a community literacy theorist, exploring how her social thought based in the concept of "socialized democracy" and symbolic interactionism might be enacted as a pedagogy; and second, to use the Hull House as a case study for assessing related challenges and opportunities in today's community literacy contexts. In particular, insights from Addams' work may resonate with instructors, both inside and particularly outside the university, who see literacy instruction as a path to civic engagement for students. While civic engagement is a notoriously contested term, I follow the Coalition for Civic Engagement and Leadership in defining civic engagement as "acting upon a heightened sense of responsibility to one's communities," which includes a variety of activities that allow "individuals—as citizens of their communities, their nations, and the world—[to be] empowered as agents of positive social change for a more democratic world" (qtd. in Jacoby 9).

Addams upheld many of these aims through her pedagogy as she linked reading and writing to social action, encouraging the mostly immigrant student population she taught to use literacy to become involved in the issues impacting their Chicago neighborhood. Her pedagogy serves as a case study of ways of approaching differences—such as race, class, language, and nationality—in the engaged community-literacy classroom. In particular, her civic engagement pedagogy both assimilated students into dominant literacies, emphasizing American language and taste, and encouraged association across social differences, promoting relationships between people of different backgrounds. I will explore how these strategies both supported and undermined her goal of social equality.

I begin by reconstructing Addams' social philosophy, discussing how this philosophy was grounded in George Herbert Mead's concept of symbolic interactionism. Mead theorized how people develop in interaction with others through symbols, a framework Addams expanded by emphasizing the role of emotion in this process. She combined this expanded version of symbolic interactionism with an ethic of democracy to create a framework for how to build a better society—and consequently, created a philosophy of education. I explain how Addams' social thought led to twin literacy pedagogies of assimilation and association. Next, I detail how each of these pedagogies was enacted at the Hull House, and I conclude with suggestions for a more rhetorical redeployment of Addams' pedagogy in contemporary community literacy programs to avoid some of Addams' pitfalls. We turn first, then, to a key term in Addams' work that I argue serves as the basis for her philosophy: socializing democracy.

Socializing Democracy

Jane Addams's autobiography, *Twenty Years at Hull House*, ends with a culminating sentence asserting that the ultimate aim of education is "to socialize democracy" (*On Education* 55). Understanding Addams' pedagogy, then, requires a journey into her social philosophy. For Addams, democracy is more than a political system; it is a set of values and a way of living. She holds to "a conception of Democracy not merely as a sentiment which desires the well-being of "all men [sic]", nor yet as a creed which believes in the essential dignity and equality of all men, but as that which affords a rule of living as well as a test of faith" (*Democracy* 7). That is, she lifts the ethics that permeate the political idea of democracy, such as equality of all citizens and access to participation, and applies these values to all of life. A belief in the dignity of all people was not a passive ideal for Addams; it required striving so that everyone could develop to full potential. Added to this ethical ideal is a "test of faith"—a pragmatic commitment to evaluating ideas solely based on their consequences when they are put into practice. Democracy is thus an attempt to manifest the concept of equality in all sectors of life through revisable practices.

How, then, is democracy "socialized?" Jane Addams never explicitly defines "socialized democracy," but one approach supported by her essay "Socializing Education" is to bring democratic ideals to social relations in the Unities States. This approach, which I term *association*, seeks to foster inclusiveness in social activities and encourage interaction between classes and races. Addams writes that learning "has to be diffused in a social atmosphere, information must be held in solution, in a medium of fellowship and good will" (*Twenty Years* 427). This fellowship extends to a diverse range of fellow humans; education should "connect [the student] with all sorts of people" (*Twenty Years* 436) and promote relationships across cultural and class boundaries.

I would like to suggest that symbolic interactionism, a line of thought developed by University of Chicago professor George Herbert Mead, may illuminate the connection between association across difference and democracy in Addams' philosophy. Mead was a close friend of Addams, often sharing meals at the Hull House and collaborating with her on reform efforts. This mutual influence extended to their philosophy; historian Mary Jo Deegan writes that links between their epistemological ties are "overwhelming" (121). Mead's symbolic interactionism posits that the self develops in interaction with others through communicative symbols. A self is comprised of an "I" who acts and a "me" who sees the self as an object and reflects on how others interpret the "I." In essence, we develop as we learn to see ourselves through the eyes of others. Therefore, the self develops the most richly when it has the opportunity to interact with a wide range of people. Diverse interaction also leads to a stronger society as it teaches people to better understand the perspectives of others—in Mead's words, to rationally "take the role of the other" (254). Echoing Mead, Addams discusses the importance of learning about the experiences of a wide range of people, asserting that "social perspective and sanity of judgment come only from contact with social experience; that such contact is the surest corrective of opinions concerning the social order, and concerning efforts, however humble, for its improvement" (*Democracy* 7). In particular, she highlights how time spent with people from different cultures plays a role in "upsetting" assumptions about the universal validity of conventions and helps people realize the situated nature of their viewpoints (*Democracy* 21).

Addams' version of symbolic interactionism parallels Mead's focus on the intellectual ability to understand the perspectives of others, but she expands his theory by emphasizing how communication allows shared feelings and an emotional understanding. Scholars have noted that Addams anticipates Carol Gilligan and Nel

Nodding's concept of an "ethic of care" (Leffers; Hamington), in which ethical motive is based not primarily on abstract conceptions of justice but on a sense of emotional connection. In *Newer Ideals of Peace*, Addams explains that ethics are grounded in compassion, and her social ethic involves extending identification beyond one's immediate group to more distant groups. Addams vividly emphasizes the crucial nature of empathy for democracy, which is developed by interacting with a range of people:

> We are learning that a standard of social ethics is not attained by traveling a sequestered byway, but by mixing on the thronged and common road where all must turn out for one another, and at least see the size of one another's burdens. To follow the path of social morality results perforce in the temper if not the practice of the democratic spirit, for it implies that diversified human experience and resultant sympathy which are the foundation and guarantee of Democracy. (7)

Associating with a variety of people fosters a sense of emotional connection with others and offers insight into different experiences and cultural logics, ultimately developing a self who is committed to the common good rather than individual interests (*Democracy* 9). Therefore, socializing democracy through association involves using interaction across social barriers to foster an expansion of perspectives and affections that leads to a wider investment in equality. The fact that this interaction occurs through language and symbols, following symbolic interactionism, holds significant implications for literacy pedagogy, as I will demonstrate in the following sections.

While the associational sense of "socialized democracy" appears to be the most common understanding of the term when it is used by Addams scholars, I suggest that another reading of "socialized democracy" is possible, especially when the term is considered in context. This understanding reads "socializing" as implicitly or explicitly training people in dominant cultural values and behaviors—teaching people to *assimilate*. Consider Addams' famous culminating sentence about socializing democracy in context of the paragraph that precedes it in *Twenty Years at Hull House*:

> The Settlement casts side none of those things which cultivated men [sic] have come to consider reasonable and goodly, but it insists that those belong as well to that great body of people who, because of toilsome and underpaid labor, are unable to procure them for themselves. Added to this is a profound conviction that the common stock of intellectual enjoyment should not be difficult of access because of the economic position of him [sic] who would approach it, that those "best results of civilization" upon which depend the finer and freer aspects of living must be incorporated into our common life and have free mobility through all elements of society if we would have our democracy endure.

> The educational activities of a Settlement, as well its philanthropic, civic, and social undertakings, are but differing manifestations of the attempt to socialize democracy, as is the very existence of the Settlement itself (452-3).

Here, in a departure from earlier parts of the essay that focused on association, Addams explicitly states that the goal of the settlement is to spread "finer" culture to new immigrants. Pierre Bourdieu's theory of habitus illuminates the dynamics of this type of socialization in relation to power. Bourdieu defined "habitus" as the taste of a particular group—their style, wit, etiquette, discriminatory ability, and expected patterns of discourse and behavior. He explains that the habitus of the dominant group, as the site of production for social normativities, becomes equated with power and refined culture and creates a designation of this habitus as "superior." Therefore, socializing democracy in this sense means equalizing society by providing underserved people access to the dominant habitus and insisting they adopt it, which, according to the logic of assimilation, allows them to stand on more equal footing with "cultivated" Americans. Of course, assimilation also enacts profound inequality by pressuring people to abandon their original cultural habitus, a form of institutional racism.

Returning to the tenets of symbolic interactionism clarifies Addams' particular version of assimilation. If the interaction needed for societal and individual development is dependent on symbols and language, it follows that a high priority will be placed on inducting immigrants into dominant American language as soon as possible. Assimilation through the lens of symbolic interactionism becomes a matter of providing access to the symbolic community, and thus opportunities for personal growth, cross-cultural understanding, and greater democracy. Yet the danger of this approach is the implications of erasing the immigrants' own symbols and language. Limiting nondominant forms of interaction alters the personal and communal development of immigrants—there is access to more than one symbolic community at stake. Addams at times recognized these dangers, and her writings are fraught with contradictions as she worked out her views on assimilation.

These two understandings of socializing, association and assimilation, reinforce and resist each other in Addams' pedagogy. We will never know which sense she intended in *Twenty Years at Hull House*. Both senses of "socializing"—relating to social activities and training in refined culture—were in circulation during her lifetime (OED), and both are present in her teaching, as I explore below. In addition, Addams herself was not a stable identity, and disconnects occurred between her philosophy and practice, between her different books and articles, and between her perspective on her teaching and what her students experienced. The interaction between these two forms of socialization and democracy is especially complicated because in some ways, assimilation is the logical underside of association given the need for common cultural codes for interaction. Yet in other ways, association positions difference as a resource to self and societal development, refuting assimilation into a single culture. The following case study of Jane Addams' pedagogy, at heart, is an inquiry into the tensions within the term "socializing democracy": how the "socializing"—assimilation and association—supports and undermines the "democracy"—social equality writ large.

Thus, these two versions of socialized democracy offer a frame for parsing out the methods and results of Addams' pedagogy and provide a starting point for exploring how a pedagogy of socialized democracy might further what many contemporary teachers, along with Addams, consider the ultimate aim of community literacy instruction: facilitating social change for a more democratic and equal world.

Association

The clashing of cultures becomes a powerfully generative force in the effort to socialize democracy through association. Such "situations of tension," for Addams, can become sites for revising attitudes and assumptions, which spur self and community growth as people encounter other ways of interpreting the world (*On Education* 210). Therefore, defying the cultural-deficit model of immigrants common at the turn of the century— and still common today—Addams writes, "We may make foreign birth a handicap to them and to us, or we may make it a very interesting and stimulating factor in their development and ours" (*Twenty Years* 410). Her pedagogy worked to create spaces for groups to co-mingle across difference through face-to-face interaction, student writing assignments, and readings about the experiences of others.

At the Hull House, opportunities for association were merged with literacy activities—often in a political context. Addams facilitated diverse English classes in conjunction with shirt-maker union meetings and coordinated discussions on current events with immigrants from a range of cultures. She emphasized the social nature of literacy learning by hosting parties for students and their families to create a sense of community in the classroom and to provide a social medium for education: "And so they learned to use English in order to play with it, so to speak. I believe that we never know a language until we have used it for social, for non-useful, non-essential purposes" (*On Education* 208). This spirit of play also brought Hull House to teach language through theater and music classes in order to develop pronunciation, reading, and fluency skills through lively performances and rehearsals.

Social association also extended beyond the Hull House neighborhood, as Addams worked to arrange cross-cultural, face-to-face exchanges between recent immigrants and upper-class Americans. For example, the Americans tutored Italians in English while learning how to cook Italian macaroni—"such a different thing from the semi-elastic product which Americans honor with that name" (*On Education* 120). This approach led to social, nontraditional spaces and postures for learning. Americans taught English to immigrant women in the kitchen, because "to learn to speak English would be a comparatively easy thing for an Italian woman while she was handling kitchen utensils and was in the midst of familiar experiences, [instead of] in the cramped, unnatural position which sitting at a child's school desk implies" (*On Education* 121). Through the power of human discourse, these social exchanges offered opportunities not only for properly *al dente* noodles and improved English conversation, but for affective relations and greater understanding between classes and cultures.

Writing offered another crucial medium for symbolic interaction across difference—an opportunity for students to present the cultural logics behind their perspectives as well as to express their emotional experiences to build bonds with the audience. Writing projects therefore at times followed what we might today term *expressivism*, as students detailed their "hopes and longings" in plays, wrote essays "outpouring sorrows," and told stories of why they decided to immigrate to America (*Twenty Years* 436). These expressivist pieces, though, were often written with a strong sense of audience and persuasive purpose. Student papers invited the audience to understand the worldview of the writer. Addams describes an essay that resonates with a pedagogy of association:

> I remember a pathetic effort on the part of a young Russian Jewess to describe the vivid inner life of an old Talmud scholar, probably her uncle or father, as of one persistently occupied with the grave and important things of the spirit, although when brought into sharp contact with busy and overworked people, he inevitably appeared self-absorbed and slothful. Certainly no one who had read her paper could again see such an old man in his praying shawl bent over his crabbed book, without a sense of understanding. (Twenty Years 437)

Pathos played a key role in bending judgmental attitudes toward a "sense of understanding" through writing, as students wrote with the goal of describing their interpretive lens and experiences to invoke emotional and intellectual comprehension. Writing served as a medium for sharing experiences and mixing on Addams' "thronged and common road," thus building democratic spirit (*Newer Ideals* 7).

Political essays written for Hull House classes also sometimes centered on explaining the experiences of people, and specifically the injustices they faced, because a purpose of mixing on the common road was to "see the size of one another's burdens" (*Newer Ideals* 7). A popular genre at Hull House, political essays covered topics such as trade unions, the single tax, and the collection of garbage (Polacheck 94). As Van Hillard explains, these essays sometimes followed "the methods of critical description associated with progressivist reform texts" (115), using sharp sensory detail to help audiences smell and brush up against the injustices that were part of poverty.

For example, Hilda Satt Polacheck authored a piece calling for food market sanitation reform during a Hull House writing class taught by Henry Porter Chandler, and she included the essay, titled "The Ghetto Market," in her autobiography. She reaches out to an audience different than her, one unfamiliar with urban street markets, writing, "Few people whose work does not take them into the neighborhood have any idea what the Ghetto market is like" (78). She proceeds to narrate her own journey to the Ghetto market, beckoning the audience toward the line of gasoline lamps that light the market, which are "nailed to the houses in an irregular line . . . like a poorly-organized torch-light parade" (78). She describes a fish merchant wearing clothing of a color now indistinguishable because of years of fish drippings as he weighs fish on a dirty scale without washing his hands. Next she visits a cake stand, where "the flies seemed very much at home ... from the constant buzzing," a situation which Polacheck notes is a likely source of typhoid fever (79). Polacheck's call to reform at the end of the essay comes after offering her audience a tour of the market, giving them a chance to understand the experiences of people in her neighborhood. Here, Polacheck is striving to open lines of communication across class barriers, and to turn knowledge about the daily lives of people that shop at the market into empathy and motivation for social change.

Addams' pedagogy of association thus anticipated what we today might call public pedagogy. She challenged the common practices of writing instruction of her time, as a majority of classroom writing occurring at the turn of the century was meant for instructors' eyes only as a private exchange and did not have the public sense of Polacheck's work (Brereton 439). Addams' philosophy of socialized democracy, in its effort to position writing as a medium for community interaction, encouraged student writers to actively wrestle with the views of a public audience.

Similarly, Addams brought the writing of others into the classroom to challenge her students to consider unfamiliar experiences and perspectives. One tactic she used to accomplish this was to spark discussion through provocative current events. She writes of how the Scopes trial prodded her students to consider the opinions of rural, religious farmers who opposed evolution, which fostered association beyond the city limits of Chicago. For Addams, placing students in conversation with prominent current events brought "into the circle of [students'] discussion a large number of people who had hitherto been quite outside their zone of interest" (*On Education* 386). Current events—which Addams describes as "molten"— melt borders and provoke association across national, and potentially even international, boundaries (*On Education* 386).

Symbolic interaction and socialized democracy also combined powerfully in the study of literature at Hull House. Addams' theory of pedagogy was implemented in the reading of fiction, as narratives offered a medium for listening to other situated perspectives and empathizing with people who have lived very different experiences. Addams writes that works of literature "satisfy an unformulated belief that to see farther, to know all sorts of men [sic], in an indefinite way, is a preparation for better social adjustment—for the remedying of social ills" (*Democracy* 8). Reading about diverse experiences can generate "a new affinity for all men [sic]" (*Democracy* 8), and Addams presents teaching literature at Hull House as one response to the violence that broke out among her neighbors (*Twenty Years* 434). Literature pedagogy thus provided a space for symbolic association and, ideally, the realignment of values to incorporate the common good.

Addams' pedagogy of association, then, focused on connecting people from diverse backgrounds so that they could interact to describe their experiences, form affective bonds, and share the reasoning behind their perspectives. As this interaction occurred through the symbolic medium of oral language and printed text, people developed their selves in response to a more diverse set of others. Therefore, ideally, they moved toward a social ethic that transferred compassion and commitment from immediate family and similar social groups outward to a widening circle of associations, and they absorbed a richer understanding of social problems through the perspectives of various social actors. Ultimately, Addams hoped to create a citizenry more equipped for effective deliberation, motivated for public problem-solving, and open to the constant revision of beliefs and practices needed for active experimentation toward the ideals of democracy.

While there are many hopeful and helpful aspects of Addams' pedagogy of association, the limitations of this approach reveal themselves with a contemporary lens attuned to the impact of power. Addams' view did not adequately take into account the highly asymmetrical power dynamics that shaped associative interaction or the ideologies that produced the experiences people described to each other. Furthermore, the fact that this utopian vision hinged on a *shared* medium of symbolic interaction pushed Addams into the highly problematic project of maneuvering Hull House participants into dominant symbolic discourses and modes, creating a twin pedagogy of socializing democracy through assimilation.

Assimilation

According to Addams, immigrant children can apply their school knowledge by "teaching the entire family and forming a connection between them and the outside world, interpreting political speeches and newspapers and eagerly transforming Italian customs into American ones" (*On Education* 81). In this quote, we see Addams' familiar commitment to association as families form connections with the outside world, and immigrant parents are able to interact with the views of others through newspapers and speeches. Yet in the same breath, Addams reveals the cultural implications of her pedagogy of socialized democracy: students are to "eagerly" change home customs into dominant ways of living—a focus on assimilation that constantly disrupted Addams' valuing of difference as a resource for self and social development.

In order for immigrant families to have access to the social sphere for association and interaction, they had to share American symbols—the English language—and have the cultural literacy necessary to make meaning of these symbols. This stance led to a Hull House emphasis on standard English, even striving "that the 'th' may be restored to its proper place in English speech" (*On Education* 152), and providing cultural literacy in the "great works" of American and British culture in reading clubs, with a special reverence reserved for Shakespeare.

Addams' focus on building democratic exchange through assimilation also led her to strongly oppose the local parochial schools, immigrant-run institutions that emphasized home language and customs as a way to keep cultural identity alive for students. For Addams, public schools were crucial sites for association between cultures and acquisition of the language necessary for interaction—a need that took precedence over the wishes of many in immigrant communities to have culturally-relevant and fully bilingual education for their children. Rivka Shipak Lissak traces Addams' multi-year battle against these parochial schools, as her tactics shifted from subtle to more overt in the attempt to redirect students toward public schools. In a particularly complex move, Addams championed home language classes in public high schools, an action that in some ways appears to be anti-assimilationist, yet in actuality was motivated by the goal of convincing parents to move their children from parochial to public education.

A generous portrait of Addams might suggest that her emphasis on dominant language and culture stemmed only from the goal of providing symbolic access. However, there is some evidence that this stance was indicative of a deeper belief that American culture was superior. Some passages of Addams' writing, especially from earlier in her career, are deeply paternalistic toward immigrant cultures. For instance, in *Democracy and Social Ethics*, Addams seems to express a view that Italian culture is less ethically "evolved" than American culture. When discussing an early stage of child morality, Addams suggests, "Primitive people, such as the South Italian peasants, are still in this stage" (101). Many Addams scholars, however, vigorously defend her against charges of cultural arrogance, dismissing passages such as this as early naiveté that Addams eventually outgrew (Deegan; Elshtain; Seigfried). As Mary Jo Deegan argues, Addams frequently expressed a strongly asset-based view of immigrant cultures, and several of her writings and actions actively resist assimilation (293).

A close examination of Addams' pedagogy reveals that she both promoted *and* resisted the assimilation of her students. Addams' conflicted approach toward assimilation makes more sense when placed in the context of symbolic interactionism. Just as Addams understood the importance of shared symbols with the wider American culture for the development of the self, she was also aware of the crucial nature of shared language and culture *within* immigrant groups for the construction of identity. She was especially "distressed" by the children of immigrants "who repudiated the language and customs of their elders" as a result of attending public school (*Twenty Years* 37). In Addams' analysis, this inability to connect with parents led to problematic self-development and juvenile delinquency (*On Education* 137). Therefore, she encouraged teachers to "take hold of [immigrants'] handicrafts and occupations, their folk songs and folk lore, the beautiful stories which every immigrant colony is ready to tell and translate . . . [and] get the children to bring these things into school" (*On Education* 140). This same impetus led Addams to develop the Labor Museum, a living showcase of immigrant craft demonstrations designed to help youth appreciate the cultural knowledge of their parents.

For Addams, then, a primary purpose of education was to integrate young people into their own culture and give meaning to their daily experiences. Though she was not aware of Gramsci's notion of local leaders as "organic intellectuals," Addams highly valued the development of educated people that stayed integrated with their families and communities. According to Addams, "The educational efforts of a Settlement should not be directed primarily to reproduce the college type of culture," but rather to increase an immigrant's ability to connect with people (*On Education* 176). Addams painted murals on the Hull House walls of leaders "who have become great through identification with the common lot, in preference to the heroes of mere achievement" (*Twenty Years* 396).

To this end of fostering leaders who identified with their home communities, the Hull House actively sought ways to bring student cultures into classes and activities. Music classes worked to transcribe and sing traditional folk songs, plays were performed in the home languages of the students, some reading classes revolved around immigrant and working class literature, and the Hull House hosted cultural celebrations.

In short, Addams' writings and actions in regards to immigrant culture are a thick tangle of contradictions; she appears to both encourage and fight the assimilation of her immigrant neighbors. Perhaps this tension lies partly in her liberal, progressive roots. As Lisa Duggan argues, one problematic aspect of liberalisms is the tendency to over-compromise in seeking a third way between radical change and reactionary forces. Addams was resisting both conservatives that claimed immigrants would degrade American culture and radical socialists calling for a comprehensive restructuring of American economics. Striving to navigate between these two poles led her into the compromise of assimilating her students.

As a reflection of her liberalism, Addams' third way involved assimilating her students into more than just pronunciation guidelines and knowledge of Shakespeare: she worked to assimilate them into dominant *political* literacies that mirrored her restraint and compromise. Ellen Gates Starr, Addams' life companion who later became a radical Christian socialist, became increasingly frustrated with Addams' emphasis on mediation. During a brutal garment strike in Chicago, Starr claimed, "Jane, if the devil himself came riding down Halsted Street with his tail waving out behind him, you'd say, 'what a beautiful curve he has in his tail'" (qtd. in Lagemann 36). In this sense, we might wonder at the version of social action Addams taught her students. To some extent, they were assimilated into habits and tastes of engagement that aligned with conservative dominant agendas. For example, in one political reading group, Addams taught Tolstoy's theories of nonresistance in response to the horrific oppression of Jewish people in the Kishinev massacre. Rather than exploring resistance, students discussed restraint.

One of the most interesting case studies of Addams' conflicting affinities with liberalism, assimilation, and democracy occurred in her attempt to turn assimilation into forms of agency for her female immigrant students. Addams sought to "teach the girls to be good mothers" by having them "study household conditions in relation to the past and present needs of the family," which is "the best possible preparation for [their] future obligations" (*On Education* 139). Furthermore, she states that young women must learn to keep house in the light of American knowledge, because immigrant mothers often hold false cultural beliefs about, for example, the reason why milk can cause disease. Addams was socializing young women into dominant American gender roles. Yet she continues in the same passage to assert, "If that girl can be taught that the milk makes the baby ill because it is not clean and be provided with a simple test that she may know when milk is clean, it may take her into the study not only of milk within the four walls of the tenement house, but into the inspection of milk in her district" (*On Education* 139-140). Here, Addams uses an identification with dominant ideals of gender to catapult immigrant women into the public sphere. Catherine Peaden claims that Addams' rhetoric that framed womanhood to include civic participation offered new forms of agency, but did so at the cost of essentializing women and submitting to the dominant frame. In other words, Addams enacted liberal feminism by arguing that women should also participate in the status quo. For Addams, assimilation and democracy were in paradox within civic engagement.

Socializing Democracy in Contemporary Community Literacy: Slowing Our Gait

Addams' pedagogy—and its complications— has many echoes in today's approaches to community literacy. Perhaps the most direct descendent is the work of the Community Literacy Center (CLC) in Pittsburgh, where Linda Flower, Wayne Peck, and Lorraine Higgins have developed an approach to teaching writing and critical thinking focused on community problem-solving dialogues. They trace their approach to the pragmatic social thought of John Dewey, who was heavily influenced by Addams (Flower). Their pedagogy brings together urban youth and college students from Carnegie Mellon University and asks them to work together to create rival interpretations of events or practices, question how different people may view the same situation, and share these interpretations in written documents and public forums. For example, participants demonstrated that while police may frame curfew laws as a safety measure, urban youth may feel unsafe in poorly supervised detention centers with adolescents from other neighborhoods, and the youth shared these perspectives at a meeting with community stakeholders including police chiefs (Deans). The Community Literacy Center uses the creation of rival interpretations as an Addamsian strategy of association, building democracy by fostering interaction between people of different social positionalities and teaching people to take on the perspectives of others. Yet as Elenore Long, David Fleming, and Linda Flower self-reflexively note, the literacy center also often encourages urban youth to take on dominant modes of reasoning such as evidence-based citation rather than the exploration of concepts through fiction (267). Also, as Tom Deans discusses, the CLC allegiance to Dewey restrains their Freirean drive toward transformative social change, as the pedagogy aims mostly toward dialogue (116). This stance—reminiscent of Addams' liberal progressivism—is illustrated in the community meeting about the curfew, which took place at the same time as a large-scale protest about police violence, drawing youth into conversation rather than political demonstration.

While the Community Literacy Center offers a remarkably robust vision of what a pedagogy of socialized democracy might look like today, we can also hear resonances with Addams' pedagogy in many aspects of contemporary approaches to literacy and civic engagement. For example, trends within rhetoric and composition call for public pedagogy and writing on public topics, and service-learning scholarship frequently celebrates the aim of fostering empathy with those who may come from different social positions.

A return to Addams' focus on association through symbolic interactionism might challenge us to reinvigorate these engaged pedagogies. She calls attention to the social and playful aspects of literacy learning, a perspective that is often overlooked in our serious attention to pressing public problems. As Addams reminds us, a key reason we learn language is to play with it and build friendships. She argues for recognition of the deeply emotional nature of linguistic and ethical development and the need to intentionally foster relationships both within the classroom and across contexts. Her theory of socializing democracy through symbolic interactionism also frames engagement with difference as an asset to self and societal development, rather than just an opportunity to develop tolerance or a chance to learn the view of the opposition so as to better refute it. In addition, she offers a strong historical precedent for incorporating home cultures and languages into community literacy instruction, and she may push us to consider nontraditional spaces and postures for education, given her drive to move students out of cramped desks and into interactive learning spaces like the labor museum or kitchen that position community members as teachers as well as learners.

Reflecting on Addams's goal of association may also prompt us to reconsider the problems of assimilation—the logical underside of associational approaches. Like Addams, today's community-literacy practitioners live in the tension between providing access to symbolic communities and defending home cultures, and the field of community literacy is as full of contradictions, shifting priorities, and unstable assertions as is Addams' work. We also may have tendencies to socialize students culturally, into dominant discourses like academic prose and standard English, and politically, into restraint and over-compromise. Yet with today's attention to power dynamics and critical theory, we may be able to rhetorically redeploy aspects of a pedagogy of socialized democracy in order to create a more empowering approach. I conclude by offering some brief thoughts toward such an endeavor.

First, a rhetorical redeployment of Addams' pedagogy requires teaching the rhetorical situation surrounding assimilation to students. Instead of simply presenting the standard discourse or offering restrained dialogue as the preferred form of civic engagement, instructors can highlight the role of power in establishing certain forms of discourse and political engagement as dominant. This path is well-trod by literacy pedagogues like Lisa Delpit, who urge us to teach standard English language and culture while positioning it in a "political power game" for students (292).

Second, a rhetorical redeployment would ask us to teach available means for persuasion beyond the dominant cultural and political methods. Culturally, instructors might bring in persuasive texts that code-switch or that are written in the home habitus of students, such as Anzaldua's *Borderlands*, now a popular text in many composition courses. Or, community literacy practitioners might follow the lead of Martha Demientieff, a Native Alaskan teacher of Athabaskan Indian youth who teaches the vocabulary and beautifully concise style of the "heritage language" alongside formal

English phrases and lengthy academic exposition. She hosts both formal dinners, where students speak standard English, and informal potlucks, where only the home language is allowed (Delpit 293).

In addition to addressing cultural assimilation, teachers also need to address political assimilation to avoid socializing students solely into forms of civic engagement that center on restrained dialogue—such as the ubiquitous letter to the editor assignment. Instead, teachers might position the civic engagement activities of the class as just one approach to social change alongside others. Minnesota Campus Compact's "social change wheel" might be a helpful tool as it depicts spokes of change that range from volunteering, to protests, to participatory action research, and to community organizing. Teachers can ask students to locate the class assignments on the wheel and discuss the merits and limitations of other approaches. Phyllis Ryder has also done work toward resisting a singular view of political engagement, suggesting that students in service-learning courses be paired with a variety of organizations to bring different views of how publics function into the classroom and to teach students to interact effectively with a variety of political logics instead of assimilating them into one approach.

In essence, the goal of a rhetorical redeployment of Addams' pedagogy would be to capture the hopeful aspects of association while better equipping students to move rhetorically within pressures to assimilate—providing a stronger sense of the rhetorical situation of assimilation and increased access to a variety of means of persuasion.

Addams recognizes that "there is no doubt that residents in a Settlement too often move towards their ends 'with hurried and ignoble gait,' putting forth thorns in their eagerness to bear grapes" (*On Education* 184). Civic engagement teachers might also be occasionally guilty of bearing thorns, especially instructors in rhetoric and composition with a "hurried gait" to join the growing movement of public composition. This is why I feel that slow, rigorous examination of our engaged pedagogies, and efforts to make these pedagogies more rhetorical, is necessary for those of us active in community literacy and civic engagement to move forward responsibly.

Addams identified her settlement house pedagogy as "a protest against a restricted view of education" (*Twenty Years* 275), and instructors who teach engaged pedagogies are part of this historic protest. It is my hope that with increased awareness of theories and precedents of pedagogies that strive toward democracy, increased attention to the associational potentials of literacy education, and increased responsibility in using symbolic interactions to address the dynamics of assimilation, we can carry on our protest with more vigor and efficacy.

Works Cited

Addams, Jane. *Democracy and Social Ethics*. 1902. Intro. Charlene Haddock Seigfried. Urbana: University of Illinois Press, 2001. Print.

———. *On Educationucation*. Ed. Ellen Lagemann. New York: Transaction Publishers, 1994. Print.

———. *Newer Ideals of Peace.* London: MacMillan, 1907. Print.
———. *Twenty Years at Hull House.* New York: Macmillan, 1910. Print.
Bowers, C.A. "The Ideologies of Progressive Education." *History of Education Quarterly.* 7.4 (Winter 1967): 452-473. Print.
Bourdieu, Pierre, and Jean-Claude Passeron. "Cultural Capital and Pedagogic Communication." *Reproduction in Education, Society and Culture.* London: Sage Publications, 1990. 71-106. Print.
Brereton, John. *The Origins of Composition Studies in the American College, 1875-1925.* Pittsburg, PA: University of Pittsburg Press, 1995. Print.
Deans, Tom. *Writing Partnerships: Service-Learning in Composition.* Urbana, IL: NCTE, 2000. Print.
Deegan, Mary Jo. *Jane Addams and the Men of the Chicago School, 1892-1918.* New Brunswick: Transaction Books, 1988. Print.
Delpit, Lisa. "The Silenced Dialogue: Power and Pedagogy in Educating Other People's Children." *Harvard Educational Review.* 58.3 (1988): 280-298.
Duggan, Lisa. *The Twilight of Equality? Neoliberalism, Cultural Politics, and the Attack on Democracy.* Boston: Beacon Press, 2003. Print.
Elshtain, Jean Bethke. *Jane Addams and the Dream of Democracy.* New York: Basic Books, 2002. Print.
Flower, Linda. "An Experimental Way of Knowing." *Learning to Rival: A Literate Practice for Intercultural Inquiry.* Ed. Flower, Linda, Elenore Long, and Lorraine Higgins. Mahwah, NJ: Erlbaum, 2000. 49-80. Print.
Gramsci, Antonio. *The Prison Notebooks.* New York: Columbia University Press, 1992. Print.
Hamington, Maurice. *Embodied Care: Jane Addams, Maurice Merleau-Ponty, and Feminist Ethics.* Ubana: University of Illinois Press, 2004. Print.
Hillard, Van. "A Place in the City: Hull House and the Architecture of Civility." *City Comp.* Ed. Bruce McComiskey and Cynthia Ryan. Albany: State University of New York Press, 2003. 128-140. Print.
Jacoby, Barbara. "Civic Engagement in Today's Higher Education: An Overview." *Civic Education in Higher Education: Concepts and Practices.* Ed. Barbara Jacoby. San Francisco: Jossey Bass, 2009. 5-30. Print.
Lagemann, Ellen. "Introduction." *On Educationucation.* By Jane Addams. New York: Transaction Publishers, 1994. Print.
Leffers, M. Regina. "Pragmatists Jane Addams and John Dewey Inform the Ethic of Care." *Hypatia* 8.2 (Spring 1993): 64-77. Print.
Lissak, Rivka Shpak. *Pluralism & Progressives: Hull House and the New Immigrants, 1890-1919.* Chicago: University of Chicago Press, 1989. Print.
Long, Elenore, David Fleming, and Linda Flower. "Rivaling at the CLC: The Logic of a Strategic Process." *Learning to Rival: A Literate Practice for Intercultural Inquiry.* Ed. Flower, Linda, Elenore Long, and Lorraine Higgins. Mahwah, NJ: Erlbaum, 2000. 255-276. Print.

Mead, George Herbert. *Mind, Self, and Society: From the Standpoint of a Social Behaviorist.* 1934. Ed. Charles W. Morris. Chicago: University of Chicago Press, 1967. Print.

Minnesota Campus Compact. "Social Change Wheel." Online video clip. *YouTube.* 5 April 2011. Web. 19 September 2012.

O'Rourke, Bridget. "Meanings and Practices of Literacy in Urban Communities: Chicago's Hull House 1880-1940." Unpublished dissertation. Purdue University, 1998. Web.

Peaden, Catherine Hobbs. "Jane Addams and the Social Rhetoric of Democracy." *Oratorical Culture in Nineteenth-Century America: Transformations in the Theory and Practice of Rhetoric.* Ed. Gregory Clark and S. Michael Halloran. Carbondale: Southern Illinois University Press, 1993. 184-207. Print.

Polacheck, Hilda Satt. *I Came a Stranger: The Story of a Hull-House Girl.* Urbana: University of Illinois Press. 1989. Print.

Ryder, Phyllis. *Rhetorics for Community Action: Public Writing and Writing Publics.* Lanham, MD: Lexington Books, 2011. Print.

Robbins, Sarah. "Domestic Didactics: Nineteenth-Century American Literary Pedagogy" by Baurbald, Stowe, and Addams. Unpublished dissertation. University of Michigan, 1993. Web.

Seigfried, Charlene Haddock. "Introduction to the Illinois Edition." *Democracy and Social Ethics.* By Jane Addams. Urbana: University of Illinois Press, 2001. Print.

"Socialize." Oxford English Dictionary Online. 2nd ed. 1989. Oxford UP. University of Arizona Campus Lib., Tucson. 20 Feb. 2009. Web.

Author Bio

Rachael Wendler is a PhD Candidate in Rhetoric, Composition, and the Teaching of English at the University of Arizona. Her research interests include community perspectives on service-learning partnerships and engaged pedagogies.

Investigating Adult Literacy Programs through Community Engagement Research: A Case Study

Jaclyn M. Wells

This article presents findings from a case study of an adult literacy program. The author conducted this IRB-approved study as part of a three-year, research-based, community-engagement project that partnered the literacy program with a writing center at a large public research university. The author argues that the participatory methods afforded by community-engagement research can allow researchers to achieve insight into particular programs while contributing to local literacy. The author also argues that understanding the characteristics of particular programs can contribute to knowledge of the field of adult literacy education and help collaborators develop engagement projects that support adult literacy.

Introduction: The Complexity of Adult Literacy

In "The Challenges Facing Adult Literacy Programs," Daphne Greenberg describes the complexity of adult literacy. She writes: "This complexity is reflected by the heterogeneity of the people who are served, the skill levels addressed, the contexts in which literacy is taught, and the settings where the programs are housed" (39). Such complexity, Greenberg argues, creates many challenges to adult literacy programs. More research about adult literacy programs could provide educators, community and university partners, and other stakeholders a better understanding of such programs and ultimately drive improvements to adult literacy education. However, the very complexity of adult literacy programs may present challenges to designing and conducting in-depth studies. Many of the characteristics Greenberg cites, such as the part-time and temporary status of instructors and students, may challenge research design and implementation. The limited resources, time, and staff of adult literacy programs may also make research difficult.

These challenges may explain the dearth of research about adult literacy programs, as well as why so much existing research relies primarily on quantitative methods that do not require long-term or significant relationships with research participants. Unfortunately, common types of research methods, such as quantitative program assessments, may not capture the full story of adult literacy education. In *Back to School: Why Everyone Deserves a Second Chance at Education*, Mike Rose argues that "second-chance" institutions like community colleges and adult education programs are often misunderstood by traditional assessment measures, and that this lack of understanding can threaten their funding, improvement, and even existence.

Case studies about specific adult literacy programs can provide a more in-depth understanding of the complex realities of adult students, teachers, and learning settings. Case study methods, however, present their own challenges, not the least being the time and commitment required of research participants. When potential research participants are as short on time and resources as teachers and administrators in adult literacy programs, qualitative methods like case study become particularly difficult. Further, high turnover among teachers and students in such programs may create challenges to engaging them in long-term studies. Even when participants in these programs are available to take part in case study research, the benefit for them and their programs may be nonexistent or trivial. Finally, researchers like university faculty may have such little understanding of these programs that they design research projects that are unrealistic or insensitive to the realities of adult literacy programs or do not benefit the teachers, students, or programs involved.

I argue that community-engagement research can address many of the challenges to designing and conducting case studies about adult literacy programs. When researchers are already engaged with an adult literacy program in a long-term partnership, they are better positioned to earn research participants' trust and design a study that is sensitive to the program's constraints and characteristics. Perhaps more importantly, research that is tied to community-engagement projects offers the possibility for the kind of reciprocity or mutual benefits discussed by service-learning scholars like Ellen Cushman and Dirk Remley. The potential for reciprocity is particularly strong when the research informs and improves the engagement project itself, thus providing a better experience, product, or collaboration for the community partner. Scholars such as Ellen Cushman (2002), Michelle Simmons and Jeffrey Grabill (2007), and Linda Flower (2008) suggest that research can improve community-university partnerships by informing program design, working toward sustainability, and investigating the effectiveness of community-engagement projects. In short, integrating research and engagement can ensure that the community partners reap the benefits of the research. Finally, the research itself may be stronger when connected to engagement, as teachers, students, and/or administrators in the adult literacy program act as active research *participants* instead of as passive research *subjects*.

As an example of such research, I offer a case study of a community adult literacy program. I conducted an IRB-approved investigation of this program as part of a three-year, research-based, community-engagement project that partnered the Purdue University Writing Lab with a local adult literacy program and a workforce-development program. I developed and sustained the engagement project for three years in collaboration with Allen Brizee[1]. I begin the article with a brief background of the engagement project to provide context for the research methodology. In the second section, I describe this methodology. I emphasize how using participatory methods and directly tying research to engagement addressed challenges to researching adult literacy programs, allowed participants to drive the research, and created a fuller picture of the program than could be gained through less participatory or less action-oriented methods. Third, I discuss the research findings, which are organized by the major characteristics of the program that emerged from a substantive analysis of the data (Maxwell 2005). While adult literacy programs are diverse, I argue that these characteristics can provide insight into the strategies, contexts, and constraints of adult literacy education.

The CWEST: A Community-University Partnership

Started in spring 2007, the Community Writing and Education Station (CWEST)[2] partners the Purdue University Writing Lab with two organizations: the Lafayette Adult Resource Academy (LARA), a local adult literacy program, and WorkOne, a state-based employment organization[3] that is locally aligned with LARA. Brizee and I began developing the project after discovering our mutual interest in community engagement, adult education, and community-based research. The project's primary result or "product" is a section of the university writing center's online writing lab (OWL) that contains free literacy materials for adult students and teachers. The materials address the three areas most commonly studied at the adult literacy program, according to LARA's teachers and administrators: the General Educational Development (GED) exam, workplace literacy and job search preparation, and English as a Second Language. Even though Brizee and I have since graduated and moved to different institutions, this adult education section of the Purdue OWL remains online and will be updated regularly by writing center staff, as the entire OWL is. In this sense, the project remains ongoing, even though the original partnership that created, researched, and revised the materials has concluded.

Based on our experiences, observations, and reading, Brizee and I approached this project knowing that many well-intentioned attempts at service learning and community engagement fail, leave community members with little benefit, and actually damage the very university-community relationships they seek to improve. When designing the CWEST, Brizee and I considered the many calls in engagement and service-learning scholarship for better community-based work. First, the project responds to arguments for sustainable, mutually beneficial, and collaborative community engagement in which university and community members exchange expertise and work toward mutual goals (Flower and Heath; Cushman; Flower). Second, the project responds to warnings about community-based work that is inappropriate to the university and community context (Grabill and Gaillet; Amare and Grettano), or that positions the community as "other" (Coogan; Edbauer). Third, the project answers calls for community engagement that is informed by research (Cushman; Goldblatt and Parks; Simmons and Grabill; Flower). We hoped that research would foster more effective collaboration between the university and community groups; we also hoped the research findings would create a better product, the adult education section of the online writing lab, for local and national use.

Perhaps most important to the CWEST is its collaborative approach to developing ideas and solving problems. In *Community Literacy and the Rhetoric of Public Engagement*, Linda Flower argues that one option for addressing philosophical and social tensions in community partnerships is to approach the work with a "spirit of inquiry." Adopting a spirit of inquiry, she argues, requires us to move beyond the postures of care and critique that have long dominated community engagement and that have cast community participants in a passive recipient role. Approaching community engagement with a spirit of inquiry respects the expertise and views of university and community participants. Thus, it allows both partners an active role in the project, which includes addressing inevitable tensions collaboratively. Flower writes that a spirit of inquiry "cannot only acknowledge some deep-running differences in how people define the problems and goals on which a collaboration is based but can embrace the difficulties of entering a cultural contact zone" (103). In the project, the spirit of inquiry—of raising and addressing questions collaboratively—pervaded the work from beginning to conclusion but was perhaps most formalized in the empirical research that informed the partnership and its products.

Community Engagement Research and Adult Literacy Programs

The study raised one major research question: What are the needs, goals, available resources, and teaching practices of teachers in the adult literacy program[4]? I sought this knowledge collaboratively with the teachers themselves to develop and improve the engagement project and its major product—the adult education section of the Purdue Online Writing Lab. The research methodology was shaped by this continuous connection between research and engagement, a connection that sparked a radical departure from traditions like researcher detachment from participants and findings. This connection meant, for example, that I had a close and ongoing relationship with the research participants, as they had been involved in the engagement project from its earliest stages. Additionally, the connection between research and engagement meant that the research participants and I had an immediate investment in the findings and their application. Specifically, we hoped that these findings would help to improve the engagement project, the OWL materials, and adult literacy education locally, all of which we cared about tremendously. The close relationship between the researcher and research participants and the mutual investment in the research findings was not simply a natural byproduct of researching an engagement project. Instead, the relationships and investment were strategic elements of the research methodology. The idea, in short, was that an ongoing, mutually beneficial relationship between the researcher and research participants and a productive connection between engagement and research would improve the research process and outcomes.

First, the research methodology was grounded by the same general philosophy of university-community collaboration that guided the entire engagement project. The methodology follows the philosophy of university-community collaboration that Strand et al. offer in *Community-Based Research and Higher Education*. The authors describe community-based research (CBR) as "a partnership of students, faculty, and community members who collaboratively engage in research with the purposes of solving a pressing community problem or effecting social change" (3). The study engages community members as collaborative research partners to solve a specific problem, the lack of free online adult basic literacy resources. This lack was a "pressing community problem," as teachers at LARA and WorkOne were limited in resources they could use to work with students. With nearly no free online resources appropriate for GED preparation, for example, the teachers were restricted to using donated materials, general online writing resources, and what few published GED preparation materials they could purchase with the program's small budget. Further, while it is beyond the scope of this article to theorize fully why free online resources for adult literacy were lacking before the CWEST, the deficiency may be due to the lower status of adult basic education and the adult students who regularly use such "second-chance" institutions (Rose). The CWEST attempted to elevate the status of these programs by including a large adult literacy section in an internationally recognized university online writing lab; in this sense, the research sought to effect social change beyond the local context. Importantly, solving the community problem and creating social change necessitated collaboration between the university and community, neither of whom had the expertise to do the work without the other.

While the broader relationship between the university and community is important to the research methodology, equally so is the relationship between the individual researcher and research participants. The research methodology is designed to avoid treating community members as research *subjects* and move toward a more collaborative research model in which the community members act as research *participants* who contribute to knowledge-making. As Ellen Cushman suggests, community-based research should parallel the engaged approach to community partnerships: if the goal of such partnerships is to work with—not for—the community, then the goal of research about the partnerships should be to create knowledge with—not about—the community. Further, the research should benefit the community members. My research methodologies follow Cushman's activist research approach— to create knowledge with the research participants, and further, to create knowledge that will benefit community members. This approach does not simply make best use of the community members' expertise (an important goal in itself) but also makes better use of the research participants' limited time. When community participants enjoy tangible benefits from research, such as improved resources or access to services, their involvement is time better spent.

The research benefitted community participants in immediate and more far-reaching ways because of its relationship with the engagement project. The research immediately benefitted community participants by providing free online instructional materials that teachers and students in the local adult literacy program could use day-to-day. Because the materials had been developed and researched with the teachers, they reflected the program's needs, goals, and teaching strategies better than materials that had been developed by outsiders. A second benefit, perhaps less immediate but equally important, is that the community participants contributed to adult literacy education far beyond the local context by using their expertise and time to develop and research the online materials. The participants, all dedicated teachers, regularly expressed pride and enthusiasm that they could contribute their expertise to help teachers and students worldwide by filling this major gap in free online adult literacy resources.

As these benefits suggest, the research was ultimately geared toward improving the community-university partnership and its products. The research methodology aligns with the model of action research described by education researcher Patricia H. Hinchey, who specifies that action research "is conducted by those inside a community" and that the research "leads to an action plan, which frequently generates a new cycle of the process" (4). Although not a member of the adult literacy program, I functioned as a community insider in the engagement project. Further, as the research progressed, the participants and I generated constant revisions to the instructional materials. We also generated and addressed new questions following Flowers' model of collaborative inquiry. Greenwood and Levin argue that action research methods like those proposed by Hinchey and collaborative inquiry proposed by Flower can improve university-community relationships. The authors argue the importance of collaboratively identifying and solving problems, as well as collaboratively assessing solutions: "Whether the 'problem' is a social/organizational or material one, the results of action research must be tangible in the sense that the participants can figure out whether or not the solution they have developed actually resolves the problem they set themselves" (150). The research methodology is grounded in this idea that action research can improve the relationship between the community and university by creating valuable knowledge with clear applications.

To investigate my research question, I conducted case studies of four teachers who volunteered for the study after Brizee and I presented at a staff meeting of the program. The case study approach follows the research model presented by Malicky et al. in "Literacy Learning in a Community-Based Program." The authors present case studies of five students in a community literacy program. Although Malicky et al. focus on students, their rationale for case study extends to adult education teachers. Like their students, these teachers are often part-time and bring diverse backgrounds and approaches to the work. Case study allowed me to gain an in-depth understanding of each instructor's perspective, and focusing on four instructors instead of just one or two allowed me to see a greater diversity of perspectives and teaching methods. Each case study consisted of interviews and teaching observations with the instructor[5]. After completing teaching observations and one-on-one interviews with all four instructors, I led a focus group with all of them to get feedback on the first online writing lab materials that were drafted, the preparation materials for the GED exam. The focus group provided a useful transition to the second round of interviews and teaching observations, which focused more directly on gaining feedback on the OWL materials. While this second round of research is not the focus of the present article, it is important to understand that the research overall was aimed at gaining information about the engagement project and its products. Finally, I collected relevant program artifacts to better understand what I gained from interviews and observations.

Data analysis also reflected a participatory approach. My major research question[6] provided the initial set of categories used to code interview and observation data: as I coded, I looked for clues about the needs, goals, available resources, and teaching practices of teachers in the program. Next, I analyzed the data further using substantive categories, which Maxwell describes as "primarily descriptive, in a broad sense that includes description of participants' concepts and beliefs" (97). Specifically, the substantive categories emerged from the major characteristics of the adult literacy program that the participants themselves identified during interviews. These characteristics also provide the organization for the section that follows. Thus, the participants not only shaped data analysis, but also the presentation of research findings.

A Picture of an Adult Literacy Program

Literacy Education as a Community Need: "An Image of Community Action and Development"[7]

The connection between literacy and community drives much of LARA's work. Findings indicate first that the program seeks to lead community improvement and second, that teachers in the program see literacy as crucial to such improvement. For the program and the teachers in it, literacy is not just about improved reading, writing, or computer skills but extends to broader social and economic issues like poverty, unemployment, crime, and drug abuse.

My first interview was with Ann[8], who at the time of the interview had taught at LARA for 30 years and also served as the program's assistant director. Like all of the teachers I interviewed, Ann commented frequently on the program's role in the community, and she argued passionately that literacy education is central to community improvement. Toward the beginning of the interview, Ann remarked: "when you're talking about language literacy, it doesn't get much more basic than that for the needs of your community. If your community is illiterate or a certain population of it is, then the whole community suffers."

Within the same conversation, Ann commented on the neighborhood surrounding LARA's building, emphasizing the area's high crime rate, the number of sexual predators and returning convicts who live there, and the prevalence of drugs:

> This...neighborhood has the most sexual predators in the city and secondly the two zip codes ----- and -----, which have the highest crime rates in this area. As well as, the highest number of folks coming out of jail and back into the community...We've got crack houses right across the street and dealers, drug traffickers right next door to us.

Despite Ann's long history in the community and program, one might question her claims, perhaps even using facts and figures to demonstrate that a neighborhood a mile away from LARA has a higher crime rate, more registered sex offenders, and a higher percentage of residents who are just returning from prison. However, the certainty of Ann's claims about the surrounding neighborhood is less important than her *perception* that the neighborhood's characteristics are relevant to the program. To Ann, it matters that LARA is situated in a troubled neighborhood, since community improvement is a central mission of the program. As Ann's remarks suggest, this mission includes addressing problems like drugs and crime through improved literacy. Ann directly stated these goals at the very end of the interview, when she said: "We would like our school building to be a beacon […] we are trying to portray an image of community action and development right here in the […] neighborhood."

LARA's official mission statement reflects this commitment to community improvement through literacy education. The mission statement reads: "In order to increase learners' capacities to make productive, ongoing changes in their personal lives, society, and public policy, our mission is to teach academic and life skills and provide for the expansion of life views" (Volunteer Training Manual). The connection between the personal and the public is important. In the official mission statement and in Ann's take on that statement, the message is the same: work at LARA does not shape individuals in isolation of each other, but instead, shapes the neighborhood and communities in which they exist. Additionally, the mission statement suggests that this work does not shape individuals in isolation from the rest of their lives; rather, it encompasses the academic, professional, and personal.

Non-Traditional Student Populations: "Our Learners Are at the Bottom"

Although specific findings about LARA's student population are beyond the scope of this study, the research does offer insight into the teachers' perceptions of the students. Findings also suggest the effect these perceptions have on the program's work. Specifically, findings suggest teachers' sensitivity to students' non-academic lives, lives that may be more complicated, challenging, and unstable than those of traditional student populations. Further, findings suggest that the program is structured to accommodate the students' lives instead of drawing firm boundaries between the academic and personal.

I return to my discussion of LARA's place and space to illustrate how the program anticipates and acknowledges students' potential personal challenges. In the previous section, I suggest that Ann's comments about the program's *place*—specifically, its location in a poor neighborhood alongside crack houses and dive bars—are significant to the program's role in the community. The program's interior—the nature of its *space*—suggests much about its student population and the program's role in their lives.

My teaching observations took place in LARA's main learning lab[9], a large room where most of the program's instruction happens. The room contains around 30 desks facing a large whiteboard, like in a typical classroom. Several computer stations, larger tables for group work, and bookshelves line the room's walls. During the teaching observations, I noted the number of flyers and posters displayed prominently throughout the learning lab. Many of these flyers and posters addressed social issues like drug addiction, while others advertised financial assistance and family programs. The front whiteboard alone displayed two posters about the dangers of methamphetamine addiction, a flyer with information about a women's crisis center, and an advertisement for a clothing drive at a local high school.

Perhaps a few anti-meth posters and some flyers about domestic violence and assistance programs do not seem that significant. However, when we compare the flyers and posters in LARA's learning lab to the flyers and posters hanging in the Purdue Writing Lab, the significance becomes clear. A visitor finds no anti-drug poster in the Writing Lab, nor does s/he find a poster with information on women's crisis support. Instead, visitors see photos of staff members, flyers advertising study abroad programs and other academic opportunities, and posters describing writing rules and strategies. The physical contrast is clear: the posters and flyers displayed in their physical space suggest that the university writing center's sphere is largely—if not solely—academic, whereas the community adult literacy program's sphere extends to the personal. Further, the more specific subjects of the many posters and flyers in LARA's learning lab suggest that the learners' personal lives are potentially influenced by such issues as drug addiction, domestic violence, and poverty.

Program artifacts also suggest that students face personal challenges that LARA teachers must acknowledge. The Individual Learner Record (ILR) provides an example. The ILR, a document used to record the student's work from the beginning of his or her enrollment at LARA, reflects many of the same issues implied by the learning lab's flyers and posters. On the ILR's first page, teachers can note if the student is a displaced homemaker, a single parent, or dislocated worker. They can also note if the learner receives public assistance, such as food stamps, Temporary Assistance to Needy Families (TANF), or refugee cash assistance. Finally, teachers are to record if the student is a resident of a correctional institution, a community correctional program, or a medical, group, or nursing home. The ILR suggests that many students in the program face financial, legal, and personal issues. That these issues are recorded in the ILR illustrates that they are viewed as relevant to the students' academic work.

During interviews, the teachers explained that many students have complicated personal backgrounds that influence their academic lives. Further, the interview findings suggest that both the program and teachers are committed to working within the context of these backgrounds. All interview participants discussed how students' personal lives influence their academic success, generally in response to questions about teaching practices and the program's day-to-day processes. When asked about her teaching practices, Ann described some potential issues that students face and commented that these issues can interfere with their studies: "I mean how can women concentrate when their kids have been taken away from them and the courts? They're facing the courts, fighting with their spouses, fighting with their landlords. You know, just a bunch of things that are going on." Ann went on to discuss the limited availability of the program's voluntary counselor, who she described as a "liaison between LARA and the community." Ann's comment substantiates her other points about the program's relationship with the community. She views the counselor as not only helping individual students but also contributing to LARA's broader goals of community improvement through literacy education. Unfortunately, the counselor's voluntary and part-time status may mean that the teachers have to act as counselors as well, a concern that was voiced by all four teachers.

The program's schedule, class structure, and enrollment are also influenced by the students' personal lives. Like many community-based literacy organizations, LARA is open entry-open exit, which means that students begin and end their work as they choose. In interviews, all of the teachers explained that financial and personal factors often interrupt students' study at LARA. The open entry-open exit system allows students to resume study when they are able. Ann articulates the philosophy behind this approach: "We are in the philosophy that we want to capture you when you can come […] So we are open entry-open exit." As Ann's comment suggests, LARA is structured so that students can come and go and that the program's very philosophy is one of accommodation with the students' lives.

Individualized, Pragmatic Teaching Strategies: "Whatever Works, Works"

Partly because of the open entry-open exit system, LARA does not hold traditional classes in which students work as a group on the same subjects. Instead, curriculum is tailored to students' specific goals and needs, and students often study independently with the teachers' input. Students come to the program for a variety of reasons, including preparing for the GED exam, developing workplace literacy skills, improving family and life skills literacy, and studying English as a second language. Since even students in the same general area will have different needs and skill levels, students in the learning lab on any given day will be studying widely different topics. Further, students come to the program with diverse learning styles, backgrounds, and attitudes toward education. The findings suggest that this diversity greatly affects teaching practices in the program and that the teachers respond to the diversity by using individualized strategies that emphasize the pragmatic or "real world."

During my observation of Alice, 26 students were present in LARA's learning lab. To begin the day's session, Alice wrote her name and the names of the three other teachers present on the board and listed five to seven student names below each of them. Alice later explained to me that she had assigned students to teachers based on their area of study. She explained that teachers work with students one-on-one in the learning lab, but working with a group of students who are all studying the same general area helps to provide some cohesion to each teacher's day.

Alice worked with six students who were preparing for the GED. The students worked independently, but she checked in regularly to monitor progress and offer help. Her interaction with one student, Sean, illustrates the degree to which regular assessment drives individualized pedagogy. When Alice sat down with Sean, she reminded him that he scored the lowest on the math portion of his practice exam. Even more specifically, she noted, he seemed to struggle with fractions. Because he was struggling with that area, Alice directed Sean to the fractions part of the Pre-GED Interactive computer program. In many interactions, Alice identified the specific area the student needed to study and directed him or her to it, just as she did with Sean.

The teachers' individualized teaching strategies stem directly from certain characteristics of the adult student population, like their busy lives, previous educational experiences, and attitudes toward school. When asked about her teaching, Alice emphasized efficiency:

> We usually start off with assessment and the students are usually pretty receptive to that because we tell them what we do and then we find out where all your needs are and you know we are going to get you through this process as efficiently as possible.

Alice's dedication to efficiency likely comes from her understanding that adult students juggle many other responsibilities and have limited time, as the Volunteer Training Manual describes. The teachers also described collaboration and transparency in lesson planning. Ann said: "I tell new people, 'Give me a week to work with you, let's try out what is best for you. Some of the things we try aren't going to work well but that tells us that this is not your style of learning.'" Creating lessons collaboratively with students and communicating openly with them may help the teachers manage the students' past experiences and attitudes toward school. Ann anticipates frustration and encourages persistence by assuring students that the strategies that do not work for them simply do not suit their learning style. Joan most directly connected individualized pedagogy with students' past problems in school by explaining, "You gotta kinda come at it with a different attitude and such because [the students] haven't been successful in the school setting. And that is why we do individualized plans."

The teachers often use a combination of directive instruction and guided independent study with students. Ann's interaction with one student, Amy, illustrates how teachers combine directive methods with independent study. At the beginning of my observation, Amy worked independently, studying for the social studies portion of the GED with an exam preparation book. While she was studying, Ann approached her briefly to drill her on multiplication tables. After Amy rattled off the "threes," Ann praised her, said they would work on "fours" next, and approached another student while Amy returned to her social studies book. After Amy had been working independently for nearly an hour, Ann approached her again. This time, she drilled Amy on her fours and then fives, and after Amy completed both successfully, Ann praised her again and said they would work on sixes next week. She then asked Amy if she would like to move on from social studies to work on keyboarding at a computer.

During my observation of Elaine, I witnessed a similar combination of directive instruction and guided independent study in teaching writing. At the beginning of the observation, one student, Sam, was doing grammar exercises on the computer. After he finished an exercise on homonyms, Elaine approached him to check his work. For each incorrect answer, she briefly explained his mistake. After providing this directive instruction, Elaine left Sam to work on his own again, this time on drafting a paragraph. Sam worked independently for nearly the rest of the observation, until Elaine approached him at the end to look at what he had written. They read over the paragraph together, and Elaine praised the strong parts of the paragraph, corrected some grammar errors, and offered suggestions for improvement. While Elaine was not working with Sam, she was walking around the learning lab working with other students, and her instruction followed a similar pattern of checking their independent work, explaining mistakes and offering encouragement, and guiding them toward further independent study.

The specific strategies teachers use often draw on students' existing knowledge and experiences. When I asked Joan to describe some of her teaching strategies, she indicated that she refers to real-world concepts to draw upon what students already know and appeal to their interests. She said: "I had one guy who doesn't like anything and it was math and it was percents. I was like, "Hey you know that CD you have in your CD player there? Don't you wanna know if you are going to the store if you are going to get a good deal? Does it say you are going to save 20%?"" The other teachers described similar strategies and emphasized the importance of tapping into students' existing knowledge, skills, and interests and building their confidence by showing them what they already know. Alice described some of the options for working with a student on the GED essay. She described many strategies that I witnessed in the learning lab, including drafting practice essays, brainstorming ideas with a tutor, and trading essays with a peer.

Elaine expressed many of the same opinions as Ann, Alice, and Joan about the diversity of teaching strategies used in the program and the importance of matching these strategies to students. However, Elaine hinted at disagreement among teachers about teaching strategies. When asked about her methods for helping students prepare for the GED essay, Elaine remarked:

> [...] we have them do the webbing first, of course because a lot of these people never think to do some kind of a quick organization of their ideas or webbing. I absolutely don't agree with the outline form that the morning [learning lab] uses. Because there is no way that you can develop such an elaborate outline when you are writing a GED [essay].

Elaine's comments remind us that, just like teachers in any context, teachers of adult literacy will not always agree on the best teaching strategies. Also interesting are the *reasons* behind Elaine's disagreement. She questions the value of teaching students outlines because she believes outlining is unrealistic in the exam's time frame. Elaine's response suggests her commitment to preparing students for a specific experience, in this case, the essay part of the GED exam. This relates to the program's mission of meeting students' individual needs, as well as the teachers' dedication to using the students' time efficiently and respecting their goals.

Variety of Resources: "We Need a lot of Things at Our Fingertips"

To support its individualized curriculum, LARA requires a variety of instructional resources. All four research participants noted during the interviews that they not only use a variety of resources, but that they actually *need* many kinds of resources at their disposal to support a diversity of student learning needs, styles, and preferences. During observations, I witnessed a variety of resources in use.

LARA's materials can be placed into a number of different categories. First, the teachers all indicated that resources include both published and teacher-created materials. Published materials include resources like textbooks and GED preparation guides. Teacher-created materials include short handouts with writing tips or sample writing. Materials can also be categorized according digital versus print. Though there are far more print materials available, the program does have two major computer programs for GED preparation: the Pre-GED Interactive and GED Interactive. Both programs are loaded onto program computers, so they do not require students to be online. A third way to categorize the available resources—and particularly the writing resources—is by whether they are directly connected to a standardized test. Many of the resources are specifically geared toward Pre-GED or GED preparation, but others cover general reading and writing skills, such as grammar and paragraphing.

All four teachers indicated that they use published materials with students, but that the resources get worn out quickly and are expensive to replace. Additionally, Alice pointed out in her interview that print resources become outdated over time. She described a paragraphing textbook that contains many paragraphs for students to model, but noted that the outdated content of the paragraphs can turn students off: "Some of the stuff that they are reading about [in the model paragraphs] is, oh my goodness, you know…you might as well be chiseling it out of stone." Despite problems that the teachers noted with published materials like textbooks and test preparation guides, these were the most commonly used resources during teaching observations.

All four teachers described using computer-based materials with students. They praised their two major digital resources, the Pre-GED and GED Interactive, for their interactivity and ability to track student work. Despite the advantages of the available GED preparation software, the instructors noted that the success of such programs depends largely upon students' comfort level with computers. In my observations, I regularly saw teachers *ask* students if they wanted to work on the computer; students were never required or even strongly directed to do so, probably because of this perspective that not all students in the program are comfortable with computers.

Interviews suggested that the choice of print or digital materials constitutes only one part of matching resources to student preferences. Alice's comments about choosing appropriate resources for the individual student are representative of many of the teachers' comments:

We find out that those tactile, kinesthetic people who are the ones who are going to be hard to stay focused are going to need more one-on-one with computer-assisted instruction. Or some of our focused, mature individuals who have strengths in reading and writing, just getting them hooked up with the right textbooks works.

Alice's comments suggest that the diversity of students who attend LARA create a need for a diversity of resources. Additionally, Alice's comments suggest that one of the teacher's major roles is to figure out what resources will be most useful to each student.

Observations support interview findings that teachers use a variety of teaching resources and that they place a high value on matching the instructional resources to students. During observations of Ann and Joan, students used Pre-GED and GED preparation books, the Pre-GED and GED Interactive software, calculators, printed practice GED tests, and scrap paper. During Elaine's observation, students used all of these resources, and one also used Microsoft Word to compose a paragraph. During Alice's observation, two students also used paragraphing textbooks that were not specifically geared toward the GED. Alice also used the official GED essay rubric and referred directly to it when offering feedback on a student's essay. Choosing resources is a collaborative process between the teacher and student, as an interaction between Alice and her student, Ned, illustrates. When Ned began his day at the learning lab, he reminded Alice that he preferred to work at the computer, and she set him up on the GED Interactive program. After Ned worked independently for an hour, Alice checked on his progress. She encouraged him to shift his focus to math, and she opened that part of the GED Interactive for him. Ned and Alice's interaction showed the process of collaborative decision-making—she allowed Ned to work at the computer like he wanted but directed him on what areas to study.

Assessments, Documentation, and Funding: "It's All about Goals and Outcomes"

A final characteristic of LARA is the importance of articulating goals and assessing and documenting progress. In observations, I witnessed that these practices form major parts of LARA's day-to-day activity, and I learned in interviews that they have both pedagogical and administrative motivations. Specifically, documenting goals and progress relate directly to the program's funding, an administrative concern, while the need for constant assessment and documentation greatly affects pedagogy.

Documenting goals and outcomes happens mainly within the Individual Learning Record that I discuss in previous sections. During every observation, I witnessed teachers regularly refer to and record in the ILR. The first page of the document asks basic demographic and contact information, employment and education status, and some financial information that I describe earlier in the article. The second page of the ILR contains student reasons for attending the program and scores for pre-tests and post-tests. The third page contains space to record the student's primary and secondary goals and achievements, as well as a section to record reasons why a student left the program if s/he left before completing the recorded goals. Finally, there is space to record multiple entry and exit dates, as well as hours of study completed on these dates.

The ILR shows how important assessment and documentation are within LARA. The major parts of the ILR indicate that a high value is placed on assessing student skill levels, articulating primary and secondary goals, and recording achievements. Furthermore, these primary goals and achievements are fairly specific: enter, improve, or retain employment; obtain high school diploma or pass GED; or enroll in postsecondary or professional education. The secondary goals are somewhat less specific and include increased involvement with children's literacy or community activities. The ILR also illustrates the program's open entry-open exit structure. This structure may make documentation even more important; since students come and go, it is essential to have a record of their work.

As LARA's assistant director, Ann has the most significant administrative role of the four participants. Not surprisingly, she had the most to say about how teachers must document goals and progress in order to keep funding. She claimed that government funding drives meticulous documentation of student skill levels, goals, and outcomes and that over the years, the documentation required to secure government funding has increased. Ann also noted that articulating goals and documenting progress is a tricky process, since the teachers feel pressure to articulate the number of goals that will produce the most desirable ratio of goals to achievements in the program's reports. She remarked: "It's so screwy because if we haven't marked a goal but we have an accomplishment, we don't get to count it." If a student gets a job while studying at LARA, for example, but did not mark "Enter Employment" on the ILR when beginning study, the program cannot report the achievement. At the same time, teachers must be careful to not mark too many goals, because the achievement quota they must meet to obtain government funding is based on a ratio of achievements met to goals articulated.

The program also uses testing to assess student learning. Again, the testing ties directly to funding. Ann described how this affects her teaching:

> [...] if we don't get level gains on standardized tests, then the government has gone to that we just don't get reimbursed. So I have that in the back of my mind as well that I want to serve their [the students'] needs and I want them to learn for the situations that they have but I also need to have them to produce on standardized tests or we don't get the money.

As Ann implies here, the administrative necessity of assessing and documenting students' progress has significant pedagogical implications. Because the students' achievements are partly measured by standardized tests and because the program's funding is based partly on these achievements, instructors like Ann may feel extra pressure to teach to the test.

Alice also discussed how the program's performance-based model affects her teaching. When asked if the program requires certain teaching methods, she said:

It's more about goals and outcomes. In adult education we do have some restrictions that we have to work around because we are performance based. So we have to emphasize learner contact hours and we have to emphasize skill development that can be measured on a standardized test. And after a certain set number of hours of instruction we need to be able to post those tests and hopefully show that the learners are getting gains in those things we diagnosed when they first came into the program.

Alice's comments remind us that even though LARA is community-based, it operates within a larger structure of national adult education. Teachers and administrators in the program focus on engaging the community, but they must also follow national and state requirements that include assessing needs and documenting goals and achievements. Her explanation clarifies that assessing student skills, identifying goals, and marking achievements have both pedagogical and administrative functions. On the one hand, determining student needs, creating study plans, and documenting progress supports individualized learning. On the other, assessment and documentation are necessary to securing funding and answering to larger stakeholders.

Conclusion

Clearly, LARA does not represent all adult literacy programs any more than one university could represent all institutions of higher education. As Greenberg argues, generalizing about adult literacy programs may be particularly difficult because the work occurs within such diverse contexts. However, LARA's characteristics may provide insight into some of the general characteristics of adult literacy education.

This insight may be useful to university and community members who are interested in collaborating with adult literacy programs. For example, prospective partners—particularly university groups—may be inclined to invite literacy programs onto their turf for events like workshops. This inclination is well intentioned, as university spaces are often larger, nicer, or better equipped than community spaces. However, LARA's mission of community action in the neighborhood suggests that university groups may do better to venture off campus and join community groups in their own space. Another characteristic, that the program needs a variety of resources to support individualized pedagogy, may have implications for the type of community engagement that will benefit adult literacy programs. For these programs, assistance with obtaining or creating resources may be a valuable result of collaboration. In a final example, service-learning participants who tutor adult students will be better equipped for the work when they understand that many adult students have complex lives and backgrounds. Service-learning students should be prepared for adult literacy groups like LARA that acknowledge the adult learners' personal challenges as part of the literacy work. These examples illustrate that collaboration with adult literacy programs is more effective when partners are familiar with the general characteristics of such groups. Further, more research about such projects can improve the engagement projects themselves and contribute to our growing knowledge of adult literacy.

Endnotes

1. The Community Writing and Education Station (CWEST) was a long-term, collaborative project that involved two separate research studies, one led by me and the other led by Allen Brizee. Further, each of those studies contained numerous stages. It is beyond the scope of this article to describe every facet of research and engagement involved in CWEST. This article will focus primarily on my case study research about the adult literacy program. For more information about Brizee's research, please see his article, "Toward Participatory Civic Engagement: Findings and Implications of a Three-Year Community-Based Research Study," published in Computers and Composition, 2014. For a discussion of how our engagement research influenced our graduate education, please see "The Engaged Dissertation: Three Points of View," by Brizee, Linda Bergmann, and me, published in *Collaborative Futures: Critical Reflections on Publicly Active Graduate Education*, 2012.

2. Even though the present article focuses primarily on my case study of the adult literacy program, some discussion of the whole engagement project is essential to understanding the research methods for the present study. Specifically, the project's overall spirit of inquiry and collaboration guided my specific research methodology.

3. In the local context, the WorkOne and LARA are closely connected. The two groups share a space in a renovated elementary school and refer students to one another. While CWEST encompassed both programs, the present study focuses primarily on LARA, the adult literacy program.

4. This article focuses primarily on the first part of my larger case study. This first part began before the online writing lab materials were drafted and was designed to provide insight into the program before Brizee and I developed the materials. The second and third parts of the research raised more specific questions about the materials themselves and how the instructors used the materials.

5. Interviews and observations were conducted before and after the development of the online writing lab materials. This article focuses on the first part of the research, so the interviews and observations that were conducted before the materials were developed.

6. What are the needs, goals, available resources, and teaching practices of teachers in the adult literacy program?

7. In this section, the second part of each heading title is a quote from teacher interviews.

8. All names have been changed.

9. One observation was conducted at the county jail, where the program holds GED classes for inmates. The county jail classroom is a unique space for instruction that clearly differs from typical academic spaces like school classrooms and writing centers. I focus primarily on the program's main learning lab in this article because this is where the majority of instruction, and the majority of my observations, takes place.

Works Cited

Condon, Frankie. "The Pen Pal Project." *Praxis: A Writing Center Journal* 2.1 (2004): n. p. Web. 25 May 2009.

Cushman, Ellen. "The Rhetorician as an Agent of Social Change." *College Composition and Communication* 47.1 (1996): 7-26. Print.

_____. "The Public Intellectual, Service Learning, and Activist Research." *College English* 61.3 (1999): 328-36. Print.

_____. "Sustainable Service Learning Programs." *College Composition and Communication* 54.1 (2002): 40-65. Print.

Flower, Linda. *Community Literacy and the Rhetoric of Public Engagement.* Carbondale, IL: Southern Illinois UP, 2008. Print.

Flower, Linda and Shirley Brice Heath. "Drawing On the Local: Collaboration and Community Expertise." *Language and Learning Across the Disciplines* 4.3 (2000): 43–55. Print.

Goldblatt, Eli and Steve Parks. "Writing Beyond the Curriculum: Fostering New Collaborations in Literacy." *College English* 62.5 (2000): 584-606. Print.

Grabill, Jeffrey T. and Lynée Lewis Gaillet. "Writing Program Design in the Metropolitan University: Toward Constructing Community Partnerships." *WPA: Writing Program Administration* 25.3 (2002): 61-78. Print.

Grabill, Jeffrey and Michele Simmons. "Toward a Civic Rhetoric for Technologically and Scientifically Complex Places: Invention, Performance, and Participation." *College Composition and Communication* 58:3 (February 2007): 419-448. Print.

Greenberg, Daphne. "The Challenges Facing Adult Literacy Programs." *Community Literacy Journal* 3.1 (Fall 2008): 39-54.

Greenwood, Davydd J. and Morten Levin. "Reconstructing the Relationships Between Universities and Society Through Action Research." *The Landscape of Qualitative Research: Theories and Issues.* 2nd ed. Ed. Norman K. Denzin, Yvonna S. Lincoln. Thousand Oaks, CA: Sage Publications, 2003. Print.

Hinchey, Patricia. *Action Research*. New York, NY: Peter Lang, 2008. Print.

Jesson, James. "Professional Development and the Community Writing Center." *Praxis: A Writing Center Journal* 4.1 (2006): n. pag. Web. 25 May 2009.

Malicky, Grace V., Herb C. Katz, Charles A. Norman, and Mary Norton. "Literacy Learning in a Community-Based Program." *Adult Basic Education* 7.2 (Summer 1997): 84-103. Print.

Maxwell, Joseph. *Qualitative Research: An Interactive Approach.* 2nd ed. Thousand Oaks, CA: Sage Publications, 2005. Print.

Remley, Dirk. "Re-considering the Range of Reciprocity on Community-Based Research and Service Learning: You Don't Have to be an Activist to Give Back." *Community Literacy Journal* 6.2 (Spring 2012): 115-132.

Rose, Mike. *Back to School: Why Everyone Deserves a Second Chance at Education.* New York: The New Press, 2012.

Strand, Kerry, Sam Marullo, Nick Cutforth, Randy Stoecker, and Patrick Donohue. *Community-Based Research and Higher Education: Principles and Practices.* San Francisco, CA: Jossey-Bass, 2003. Print.

Author Bio

Jaclyn M. Wells is an assistant professor of English and writing center director at the University of Alabama at Birmingham. Her research interests include writing center administration, community engagement, and public rhetoric. Jaclyn's introductory and professional writing courses often include community-based projects. In one such project, Jaclyn takes students to an inner-city elementary school in Birmingham to lead writing workshops for third- and fourth-grade students; at the completion of these workshops, the professional writing students design and print an anthology of the children's work.

Reading Under Cover of the Veil: Oral and Textual Literacies in Antebellum America

Sandra Elaine Jones

This article examines the relationship between oral- and textual-literacy systems that existed during the antebellum period of United States history. I argue that African-American intellectual processes are more accurately understood as existing on a literacy continuum that reflects equality between oral literacy and textual literacy. A literacy continuum deconstructs the notion of the textual supremacy and assumes a mutually dependent relationship between the oral and the textual. Ultimately, it enables a reevaluation of oral practices as intellectual processes and systems of knowledge production.

> Leaving...the world of the white man, I have stepped within the Veil, raising it that you may view faintly its deeper recesses,—the meaning of its religion, the passion of its human sorrow, and the struggle of its greater souls.
> —W. E. B. Du Bois, *Souls of Black Folk*

Introduction

Elizabeth McHenry's "Forgotten Readers: African-American Literary Societies and the American Scene" examines black female literary societies that existed in free black communities in the nineteenth century.[1] Literary societies were established in significant numbers in the 1800s and served a vital educational function in black communities for nearly 100 years. Yet, this historical phenomenon has received little scholarly attention. McHenry maintains that because of this serious scholarly neglect, "we remain less cognizant of the variety of processes of intellectual production and exchange that have existed within African-American communities--processes through which texts were both created and read" (150). McHenry attributes this neglect to the singular identification of black culture as "oral in nature." Such a characterization, she argues, has obscured the full scope of black intellectual processes, especially the reading and writing of texts (151).

While McHenry argues that the identification of black culture as oral in nature has obscured our understanding of African-American intellectual processes, I believe the characterization of African Americans as an "illiterate race"—from the early seventeenth century through much of the twentieth century—constitutes a greater problem. The illiterate label in relationship to African Americans is problematic because it assumes a European-based written textuality as the exclusive and universal standard by which knowledge is produced and measured. In other words, it suggests that a European-based textual literacy is the only valid form of literacy that exists and the only important literacy for African Americas to acquire. However, this assumption ignores the very real conditions under which African Americans existed in the Americas. It denies the rich intellectual production and exchange rooted in oral knowledge production systems. The existence of perpetual enslavement where participation in activities like reading and writing were often prohibited by law required the utilization of alternative forms of intellectual development and exchange. Oral traditions were vitally important under these circumstances. For example, storytelling, the verbal transmission of knowledge, proved to be a central mechanism by which family and cultural history was preserved and passed along the generations. Music, the simple singing of spirituals or blues, became powerful communication mechanisms for enslaved African Americans. The creation of meaning through behavior provided an alternative means of intellectual exchange. Under the conditions of enslavement, acquiring literacy of these alternative oral forms was often more important than textual literacy.

Like the authenticity arguments that surrounded early black literary production, the assumption that blacks are an illiterate race is an outgrowth of the fallacy of black inferiority. An idea rooted in the social construction of the slave persona, the designation as inherently illiterate was an important feature of the dehumanization of black people. Such a broad characterization implied that, with just a few exceptions, blacks as a race have limited intellectual capabilities that impede a significant mastery of intellectual practices, including written literacy skills. Moreover, black inferiority theories imply that these intellectual constraints are inherent in the physiological makeup of the black body. In this context, illiteracy becomes synonymous with educability and suggests that African Americans as a population are not "educable." This designation has persisted over time, during periods of enslavement as well as freedom, and manifests itself in modern biological and cultural determinist theories such as those authored by Arthur Jensen (*Genetics and Education*), and Richard J. Herrnstein and Charles Murray (*The Bell Curve*). In actuality, rather than proving genetic and biological inferiority, these pseudo-scientific theories serve to legitimize any societal inequalities or disadvantages suffered by African-American populations.

Understanding the full scope of African-American intellectual processes of which McHenry speaks requires a recognition and re-evaluation of other knowledge production systems, especially oral ones. I argue in this article that African-American intellectual processes are more accurately understood as existing on a literacy continuum with an equal level of utility for both oral literacy and textual literacy. Situating knowledge production in an oral context expands the definition of literacy and challenges the superiority of Western concepts of literacy that construct a binary between the textual and the oral. The written/oral binary assumes a dominant/subordinate power relationship between textual literacy and oral literacy. A literacy continuum deconstructs the notion of the supremacy of textual literacy and assumes a mutually dependent relationship between the oral and the textual. At the same time, a literacy continuum enables a re-evaluation of orality as a valid intellectual process and system of knowledge production. A literacy continuum leads one to the genesis of African-American intellectual processes found in antebellum America, particularly in the everyday survival existence of the enslaved population. Intellectual as well as physical survival depended on mastery of uniquely constructed knowledge generating systems rooted in African knowledge production systems. Without the construction of an orally-based system, black resistance to slavery would have been impossible.

Critical Literacy Theory

Particularly relevant to this topic is the emerging field of "New Literacy," or critical literacy studies that challenge traditional Western definitions of literacy, as too narrow to encompass the full range of literacy practices.[2] Critical literacy studies offer a decidedly different conceptual frame that views literacy in broader sociocultural and political terms by recognizing how language is affected by and effects social relations. As such, language contains a value specific to the circumstance in which it is used. It follows that acquiring language literacy—written and oral—is relevant only in the context in which it is needed and practiced.

My argument assumes that a temporally, geographically, and culturally affected term such as "literacy" is best examined recognizing the elusiveness of its definition as a concept and practice. A traditional definition of literacy is "the quality or state of being literate" (Merriam-Webster). In its most practical Western sense, literacy has generally meant obtaining the ability to read and write. Yet, the level of reading and writing skills one needs to be considered literate has undergone many changes over time. For the great majority of the population in the British-American colonies for most of the eighteenth century, the "quality or state of being literate" meant acquiring very basic skills in reading primarily for the purpose of religious instruction. Writing, or more precisely penmanship, was considered an advanced skill until the 1830s (Thornton 76). In the antebellum period, the ability to sign one's name was a significant measure of literacy. With the growth and mass accessibility of American public education in the late 1800s,[3] enrollment in school became the method by which literacy levels for the population were measured. Many argue that today's "state of being literate" should include the new literacy associated with the technological era since computers, the internet, emailing, texting, and tweeting have become central media in information and communication dissemination. Under such fluid socially constructed standards, the quality or state of being literate, then, depends largely on the societal context.

Contemporary scholarship across a spectrum of disciplines challenge the boundaries of traditional definitions as too limited to consider temporal, geographic, and cultural changes affecting concepts and measurements of literacy. For example, Dubin and Kuhlman discuss literacy in a broader academic context by suggesting the literacy has come to encompass meanings that go beyond the simple definition of reading and writing to include competence, knowledge and skills (v-x). Sociologist J.A. Langer argues for a more comprehensive definition suggesting that, "literacy can be viewed in a broader and educationally more productive way, as the ability to think and reason like a literate person, *within a particular society*" (9-27). Anthropologist James Collins challenges limited literacy definitions by questioning the "central assumptions that literacy can be treated as a thing-in-itself, as an autonomous technology... its nature and meaning shaped by, rather than determinate of, broad cultural-historical frameworks and specific cultural practices" (75-93).

In her study of the African-American literacy practices in the modern American classroom, Elaine Richardson identifies a conceptual incompatibility between African-American Vernacular English and the historical propensity for schools to promote what she terms "White supremacist and capitalistic-based literacy." She argues that the diverse composition of modern American classrooms requires an expanded use of language and literacy forms. Effective teaching and learning of African-American students require an expanded use of African American Vernacular English, noting the ways in which African-American literacy practices has been an essential attribute to African American survival from "slave ship to scholarship" (4). Richardson's findings underscore a general argument that context is as essential for assessing literacy as it is for understanding and interpreting African-American intellectual processes. It also attests to the importance of considering a range of oral practices as significant forms of literacy and knowledge production.

Influenced heavily by critical literacy approaches, I argue that within the cultural-historical framework of a society which Abraham Lincoln called half free and half slave (Lincoln "A House Divided"), where the enslaved population was subjected to laws that prohibited acquisition of written literacy, mastering the skills of oral literacy constituted the most essential attribute of the "quality or state of being literate" for African Americans. Unique cultural-historical conditions necessitated the simultaneous construction of an alternative oral literacy system at the same time as blacks attempted to acquire textual literacy skills. An alternative literacy system grew largely "under cover of the veil"—that is, outside of the literacy framework of the dominant white population. Furthermore, this alternative literacy was grounded epistemologically in the oral traditions culturally specific to African cultures. Thus, an exploration of African-American literacy during the slavery era must take into consideration a range of oral practices that were developed and used by the enslaved population, which traditional definitions do not allow. Practices such as memorization and forms such as storytelling, spoken-word poetry, blues-song constructions, sermons, and testifying all became important components of the analytical skill sets that functioned as methods of producing knowledge.

Oral Literacy

I have argued that reading and writing were not the only forms of literacy necessary for enslaved Africans in antebellum America. Oral literacy also held significance in creating unique African-American communication systems vital to black progress and survival under slavery. In fact, the state of being literate for the enslaved population meant being intimately familiar with those systems. Storytelling, testifying, songs, riddles, and more were rooted in oral traditions that derive from the culture that Africans carried with them from Africa. Orality constituted an accessible and democratic mode of teaching and learning in black communities that were available to all; at the same time, it provided a protective shield from intrusion by white society, and, as Heather Williams suggests, provided a private life for enslaved Americans (7). Williams maintains that most of the news and information gathered by the enslaved involved "listen[ing] hard and remember[ing] well." She writes that eavesdropping

> Constituted a vital and accessible component of the intelligence network within slave communities. As important as literacy was to the slaves who employed it in service of their own freedom or for the benefit of others, enslaved African Americans also had other ways of knowing. They relied heavily on oral and aural systems of information. (9)

Other "ways of knowing" such as listening, information gathering, memorization, and articulation skills facilitated learning in an environment that forbade it. Orality made it possible to pass on information and knowledge from person to person and from one generation to the next. It provided collective analytical forms through which blacks could make sense of and affect the world around them. Because orality is a participatory activity, it helped to create community linkages and a sense of identity as well.

Drawing upon oral traditions, enslaved blacks devised their own secret communication systems that only they were effective in decoding. Encrypted messages embedded in songs, hidden in quilts, and incorporated in riddles are all examples of an underground communication system existing in slave communities. The roles of music and song in the daily lives of enslaved populations are well documented (Genovese; Blassinggame; Southern). Because many forms of communication, including group conversations, were often forbidden by slavocrats, singing was among the few collective activities in which blacks could engage freely. Angela Davis observes that music became an extension of everyday speech serving both an aesthetic and political purposes. Davis notes that, "the musicalization of speech" became a means of "preserving African cultural memory," as well as "help[ing] to construct community among the slaves." She writes:

> Through field hollers and work songs, black people communicated to one another a sense of membership in a community that challenged their collective identity as slaves. They created a language whose meanings were indecipherable to everyone who was not privy to the required code. And, indeed, white slave owners and overseers often assumed that work songs revealed an acquiescence to slavery…The language of spirituals…was encoded in a way that permitted slaves to communicate specific modes of resistance through metaphors based on biblical teachings. (167)

Spiritual music, as well as other cultural attributes, represented a masterful method of resistance, especially in the countless individual and collective efforts to escape a life of enslavement. Music served as a medium through which messages circulated throughout the enslaved community when a planned escape was underway. They contained instructions on when to leave and maps of where to go to be safe from detection. These very practices represent communication systems that were hidden in plain view. They were available to those able to understand them and unavailable to outsiders.

Frances Harper's *Iola Leroy*, one of the first known novels written by an African-American woman, contains illuminating examples of the hidden communication system that existed among the enslaved community. Although it is a fictional account, it is illustrative of the type of hidden communication systems based on oral traditions. In its opening pages, Harper introduces the concept of "market speech," a covert means of communication that existed in the novel's slave community. *Iola Leroy* begins with a seemingly simple dialogue between two of the novel's main characters, Robert Johnson and Tom Anderson, who appear to be discussing the quality of produce in the market. Both characters are slaves, and the time is set toward the end of the Civil War.

"Good mornin', Bob; how's butter dis mornin'?"

"Fresh; just as fresh, as fresh can be."

Did you see de fish in de market dis mornin'? Oh, but dey war splendid, jis' as fresh, as fresh can be."

"That's the ticket," said Robert as a broad smile overspread his face. (Harper 2)

We learn shortly that this simple dialogue contains a hidden message of significance. The state of the market is a metaphorical reference to the successful efforts of the North in the Civil War. Harper soon tells us "some of the shrewder slaves, coming in contact with their masters and overhearing their conversations, invented phraseology to convey in the most unsuspected manner news to each other from the battle field" (8-9). The obvious intention of this dialogue in market speech is to introduce the existence of an alternative form of literacy among the novel's slave community that figures significantly in the novel's construction.

By introducing market speech in the beginning of the story, Harper provides an important instruction to its readers on how to gain meaning from the novel as a whole. P. Gabrielle Foreman's concept of "histotextuality" is useful for explaining the function of the type of market speech found in *Iola*. Histotextuality or "surplus meanings" is a covert correlation between a text and historical events or figures that have become a part of a group cultural frame of reference. Foreman explains that it is "a strategy marginalized writers use to incorporate historical allusions that both contextualize and radicalize their work by countering the putatively innocuous generic codes they seem to have endorsed" (330). While the story in *Iola* is written using the popular sentimentalist style of the nineteenth century, the cultural referents in the novel are the historical references that come from a decidedly African-American experience and black historical-cultural context. The significance of the Civil War, the inclusion of characters modeled after important figures in black history such as W.E.B Du Bois and Booker T. Washington, and references to specific issues such as the surreptitious acquisition of education are significant identifiers for a black reading audience. While Harper appears to address one audience with her use of sentimentalism, her historically based rhetorical strategy is in fact a covert communication with another audience—itself a form of market speech.

In *Iola Leroy*'s black community, information is gathered and shared in ways that make use of alternative literacies. Information comes from newspapers, as well as through listening to conversations, or as Williams's terms it, "ease dropping." Body language and other everyday behaviors is also a part of information gathering that introduces another kind of literacy. For example, the light and happy demeanor of Bob and Tom in the passage cited above is a behavior that can be read as a text. It becomes an indication to those who can interpret it that the North is doing well in the war. Harper gives a very explicit demonstration of the literacy of reading behavior through the character Linda. After his encounter with Robert, Tom enters his home and begins to relate to Linda the news that he has learned that day. He tells her that the papers are full of news about the victories of the North, to which Linda replies:

> Oh, sho, chile…I can't read de newspapers, but ole Missus' face is newspaper nuff for me. I looks at her ebery mornin' wen she comes inter dis kitchen. Ef her face is long an' she walks kine o' droopy den I thinks things is qwine wrong for dem. But ef she comes out yere looking might pleased, an' larffin all ober her face, an' steppin' so frisky, den I knows de Secesh is gittin' de bes ob de Yankees. (9-10)

Linda has devised a way to read and interpret the fortunes and misfortunes of war through the behaviors and moods of "ole Missus." In this situation, the behaviors and moods of the oppressing class provide just as much information as the newspapers. How very important this form of literacy must have been to slaves. With these different literacies in oral as well as written forms, all in the community possess the ability to effectively read and interpret important situations and events relevant to the survival of blacks.

These simple dialogues suggest much about the multiple literacy forms used in the conduct of everyday life in slave communities. Our first speaker Tom speaks in dialect, which Harper uses to represent that he cannot read or write. Robert, on the other hand, speaks Standard English, and Harper tells us that he has learned to read and write. Yet, these two speakers communicate in a third way that is accessible to both of them but not readily accessible to the slave-owning white population around them. Market speech, the coded language of resistance, is a valued language medium in this situation. It requires a different literacy developed by the community for the purpose of safely exchanging knowledge and giving meaning to events. One can imagine many instances where market speech or a subtext, oral reading, and relationships between the written and spoken word were used to conduct the business of the slave community. The ability to participate in this covert communication system depended on knowledge that of necessity was transmitted orally from one generation to the next. Orality aided secrecy, which was especially important in regard to the resistance of slaves to their bondage.

Orality, existing as it did in the center of antebellum African-American life, occupied an essential space in the African-American intellectual tradition. Moreover, it maintained a vital connection between the African cultural past and the African-American cultural present. Orality represented an immediately accessible vehicle for African diasporic cultural survival in the Americas. In this context, it was perhaps initially more important than the textual communication forms that blacks would grow into.

Oral and Textual Literacy Continuum

This is not to deny the importance of textual literacy for the enslaved populations. However, traditional literacy scholarship fails to explore these two systems on a continuum and consequently obscures the significance of oral literacy practices. Oral communication forms had a utilitarian function that actually facilitated the acquisition of reading and writing literacy.[4] The typical methods of teaching reading in antebellum America gave a great advantage to those with a high level of oral learning skills. To acquire this elementary level of literacy, one simply needed to hone the ability to "listen hard" and "remember well." A more useful practice is exploring the continuum of oral and textual literacy during the period of American slavery. I begin with the assumption that the "state or quality of being literate" is determined to a large degree by societal context. The state or quality of being literate was different for blacks not only because of the oral influences in their culture. The condition of enslavement required mastering a variety of literacy forms that included reading and writing skills, and it necessitated alternative forms of communication based in oral traditions. Therefore, any accurate assessment of African-American intellectual development, especially during the slave era, must necessarily include literacy rooted in oral traditions as a learnable and viable structure.

It is helpful to remember that enslaved populations in the colonial and antebellum eras existed within a society that was itself embracing Enlightenment principles of rationality. African Americans were inspired by Enlightenment principles precisely because they included the ideals of freedom and equality for all human beings. In this context textual literacy held an ideological as well as a practical allure for black people. The second part deals with the importance of retention of oral traditions rooted in indigenous knowledge production methods that enabled cultural development and physical survival. In this context orality and textuality represents two different but equal ways of knowing. Blending these two systems establishes a continuum unique to African-American culture. Labeling African Americans as belonging to an illiterate race ignores the extensive and most often surreptitious reading instruction available to blacks that existed for the entire length of the chattel slavery era. Recent scholarship has raised questions about the levels of textual illiteracy among enslaved black Americans during the colonial and antebellum eras.

For example, E. Jennifer Monaghan's *Learning to Read and Write in Colonial America, Studies in Print Culture and the History of the Book* includes an exploration of the multitude of individual and institutional avenues to reading and writing literacy available to African Americans in the colonial and the antebellum periods of American history. Janet Duitsman Cornelius's *When I can Read My Title Clear: Literacy, Slavery, and Religion in the Antebellum South*, suggests that more blacks than we have previously acknowledged did, in fact, acquire reading and writing skills. She questions the extent and effectiveness of anti-literacy laws in preventing African Americans from acquiring reading and writing skills. Heather Andrea Williams' *Self-taught: African American Education in Slavery and Freedom* examines the learning process of enslaved people and shows the use of oral literacy as a means of resistance. In the process, Williams illuminates the central role of orality in the life of the black populations and its importance in the acquisition of textual literacy.

Testimony taken from ex-slaves and slave narratives describe the ways in which oral processes aided in the acquisition of textual literacy among enslaved populations and suggests a much larger textually literate population than previously recognized. Because orality was an integral component of African-American culture, these processes were easily employed. Virginia-born ex-slave John Quincy Adams reported,

> Whenever he heard a white person reading aloud, he lingered to listen… Then, at the first opportunity, he repeated to his parents everything he had heard. They, in turn, encouraged him to "try to hear all you can, but don't let them know it. (Williams 9)

Most importantly, a spoken reading lesson could not be easily discovered by whites. Instruction that began by listening and remembering was continued by articulating and decoding what was remembered in the privacy of slave cabins.

In another example, "A woman in Beaufort, South Carolina, recalled that her mistress and master spelled out any information they did not want her to understand. As she was unable to read, she memorized the letters and repeated them as soon as she could to her literate uncle. He then decoded her memories into words or scraps of words (Williams 9)." Interestingly, Williams has found that, "more than one hundred years [after slavery], when slave cabins were excavated, archaeologists were surprised to find, along with predictable shards of colon ware pottery, food bones, and oyster shells, the remains of graphite pencils and writing slates, some with words and numbers still written on them (20-21)."

Basic literacy instruction can even be found in the games of enslaved children. In a 1989 article on the playing habits of slave children, David K. Wiggins describes children's games that demonstrate how such a process might have gone. His information is taken from 1930s WPA interviews conducted with ex-slaves:

> Through the playing of games, slave children were often able to learn simple skills of literacy. "I learned some of the ABC's in playing ball with the white children," remembered Mattie Fannen of Arkansas. Anna Parks, who lived on a large plantation in Georgia, remembered nothing about special games except "Old Hundred." "Us would choose one and that one would hide his face against a tree while he counted to a hundred. Then he would hunt for all the others. They would be hiding while he was counting. We learned to count playing Ole Hundred. (25)

While these examples show the use of memorization skills in obtaining information, they also illustrate the communal nature of the learning process. More importantly, they show how it was possible to safely pass these skills from one generation to the next through the conduct of everyday work and play.

The preceding examples illustrate the strong relationship between oral and written literacy in the everyday lives of enslaved people. They show a literacy continuum at work in which one form facilitated the other. As a community, blacks understood well the value of oral and written literacy as a survival skill, and as a community, they handed down the craft to younger generations using methods that were best suited to their acquisition. Blacks who learned to read taught other blacks. They read letters and newspapers to those who could not read themselves. In this sense, if one person on a plantation or in a town could read and write, oral practices gave the entire community access to written literacy. Consequently, rather than replacing other forms of literacy, written literacy complimented orality, and the two function together as a literacy continuum.

Exploring literacy on a continuum enables one to articulate a more complete picture of African-American intellectual life during the period of American slavery. Erasing the textual versus non-textual paradigm allows recognition of the unique intellectual processes located at the center of African-American life. It affords an opportunity to look under cover of the veil into the intellectual life and processes of enslaved populations, and it revalues those processes. Thus we are positioned to consider some of the long neglected processes of intellectual production and exchange of which McHenry speaks. While McHenry's argument relies on the position that the characterization of African-American culture as oral in nature has been emphasized too much, I think a reconsideration of oral practices examining them in relation to textual literacy could broaden our understanding of those processes.

Endnotes

1. This article became a chapter in McHenry's *Forgotten Readers: Recovering the Lost History of African American Literary Societies* published in 2002.

2. The concept and practice of critical literacy grew out of the social justice pedagogy of Brazilian Marxist educator Paulo Freire.

3. For example, free public elementary education was available to all American children

by the end of the 19th century. The 1862 Morrill Act or the Land Grant College Act enabled the creation of colleges in the states.

4. According to Monaghan, for most people literacy was measured by the ability to read on elementary levels and to sign one's name. Formal schooling was not necessary. Typical instruction in reading followed the "'ordinary road,' a tiered process beginning with the alphabet, four lines of syllables, the invocation, and the Lord's Prayer and ending with the Bible. Reading texts was most often slow and deliberate, and was oral in nature with lessons taught by rote."

Work Cited

Bassard, Katherine Clay. "Gender and Genre: Black Women's Autobiography and theIdeology of Literacy." *African American Review* 26, No. 1, Women Writers Issue (1992): 119-129.

Blassingame, John W. *The Slave Community: Plantation Life in the Antebellum South* (1972; rev. ed., New York: Oxford University Press, 1979.

Collins, James. "Literacy and Literacies." *Annual Review of Anthropology* 24, (1995): 75-93.

Cornelius, Janet Duitsman. *When I Can Read My Title Clear: Literacy, Slavery, and Religion in the Antebellum South*. Columbia, S.C.: University of South Carolina Press, 1991.

Crafts, Hannah. *The Bondwoman's Narrative*. Henry Louis Gates, ed. New York: Warner Books, 2002.

Danky, James Philip, and Wayne A. Wiegand. *Print Culture in a Diverse America, History of Communication*. Urbana: University of Illinois Press, 1998.

Davis, Angela Y., *Blues Legacies and Black Feminism: Gertrude "Ma" Rainey, Bessie Smith and Billie Holiday*. New York: Vintage, 1999.

Douglass, Frederick. *Narrative of the Life of Frederick Douglass, an American Slave.* Cambridge, Mass., Belknap Press, 1960.

Dubin, F., & Kuhlman, N. A. (1992). The dimensions of cross-cultural literacy. In F. Dubin & N. A. Kuhlman (Eds.). *Cross-cultural Literacy: Global Perspectives on Reading and Writing* (pp. v-x). Englewood Cliffs, NJ: Regents/Prentice Hall.

Du Bois, W. E. B. *The Souls of Black Folk*. Chicago: A.C. McClurg & Co.; [Cambridge]: University Press John Wilson and Son, Cambridge, U.S.A., 1903; Bartleby.com, 1999.

Foreman, P. Gabrielle. "'Reading Aright': White Slavery, Black Referents and the Strategy of Histotexuality in *Iola Leroy*." *Yale Journal of Criticism*, Fall 1997.

Gates, Henry Louis. *Figures in Black: Words, Signs, and the "Racial Self."* New York and Oxford: Oxford University Press, 1987.

Genovese, Eugene D. Roll, *Jordan, Roll: The World the Slaves Made*. (1972; New York: Vintage Books, 1976).

Harper, Frances Ellen Watkins. *Iola Leroy, or Shadows Uplifted, Schomburg Library of Nineteenth-Century Black Women Writers*. New York: Oxford University Press, 1988.

Hernstein, Richard J. and Charles Murray. *The Bell Curve: Intelligence and Class Structure in American Life*. New York: Free Press Paperbacks, 1994.

Jensen, Arthur Robert. *Genetics and Education*. [1st U.S. ed. New York, Harper & Row, 1972.

Johnson, J.A., Collins, H.W., Dupuis, V.L. and Johansen, J.H. *Introduction to the Foundations of American Education*, Sixth Edition. Allyn and Bacon, Inc.,1985.

Kennedy, Michael V., and William G. Shade. *The World Turned Upside-Down: The State of Eighteenth-Century American Studies at the Beginning of the Twenty-First Century*. Bethlehem [Pa.] London; Cranbury, NJ: Lehigh University Press; Associated University Presses, 2001.

Langer, J. A. (1991). Literacy and schooling: "A Sociocognitive Perspective." E. H. Hiebert (Ed.), *Literacy for a Diverse Society: Perspectives, Practices, and Policies*. New York: Teachers College Press, 1991.

Lincoln, Abraham. *Speeches & Letters of Abraham Lincoln, 1832-1865*. London: J.M. Dent & Co.; New York, E.P. Dutton & Co., 1907.

McHenry, Elizabeth. *Forgotten Readers: Recovering the Lost History of African-American Literary Societies*. Durham and London: Duke University Press, 2002.

Merriam-Webster's Collegiate Dictionary online (www.m-w.com/cgi-bin/dictionary).

Monaghan, E. Jennifer. *Learning to Read and Write in Colonial America, Studies in Print Culture and the History of the Book*. Amherst Worcester: University of Massachusetts Press; American Antiquarian Society, 2005.

Richardson, Elaine. *African American Literacies*. London: Rutledge, 2003.

Snyder, Tom, ed. *120 Years of American education: A Statistical Portrait*. National Center for Education Statistics, 1993.

Southern, Eileen. *The Music of Black Americans: A History'*. W. W. Norton & Company; 3rd edition, (1997).

Thornton, Tamara Plakins. *Handwriting in America: A Cultural History*. New Haven, CT: Yale University Press, 1996.

Wiggins, David K. "The Play of Slave Children in the Plantation Communities of the Old South, 1820-1860." *Journal of Sport History*, Vol. 7, No. 2 (Summer, 1980).

Williams, Heather Andrea. *Self-Taught: African American Education in Slavery and Freedom*. Chapel Hill: University of North Carolina Press, 2005.

Woodtar, Dee Parmer. *Finding a Place Called Home: A Guide to African-American Genealogy and Historical Identity*. New York: Random House, 1999.

Author Bio

Sandra E. Jones is an assistant professor in the Department of Africology at the University of Wisconsin-Milwaukee. She teaches African-American literature, African-American literary criticism and theory, and black feminist criticism.

"To Learn About Science": Real Life Scientific Literacy Across Multicultural Communities

Adriana Briseño-Garzón, Kristen H. Perry, and Victoria Purcell-Gates

Much of the current research on scientific literacy focuses on particular text genres read by students within the classroom context. We offer a cross-case analysis of literacy as social practice in multicultural communities around the world, through which we reveal that individuals with no formal education, as well as people with varied levels of schooling completed, customarily and actively engage in literacy events with the goal of learning about science as part of their everyday lives. We argue that these outcomes substantiate the notion that multiple ways of being scientifically literate actually exist and that scientific literacy in its most fundamental sense is crucial in science education, despite the fact that the most common definitions and notions of scientific literacy have predominantly considered its derived sense (Norris and Phillips 224).

Introduction

Many definitions and approaches to science or scientific literacy have been set forth by institutional authorities, educators, and researchers from varied fields of study, such as science education, disciplinary literacy, and social research on public engagement with science (AAAS; Hand et al.; Lemke). Different disciplinary takes on science education and literacy have yielded distinctive interpretations of terms, theoretical perspectives, lines and methods of research, as well as relatively independent bodies of knowledge around a common topic (Feinstein). The analysis we present here is theoretically framed by two converging fields of inquiry: science education and disciplinary literacy.

Science educators and science-education researchers rather indistinctly use the terms science literacy and scientific literacy as interchangeable. According to Roberts (732), the term *scientific literacy* predominates in the literature and is pervasively used in a number of countries. *Science literacy*, on the other hand, is particularly utilized by science educators in the United States as a result of its appearance in the official documents published by the American Association for the Advancement of Science in 1990 and beyond (Roberts 732). For many researchers the discrepancy has no implications, although some consider that the terms differ in meaning. Considering that researchers in the literacy field have also consistently made use of the term scientific literacy in their investigations and reports, we have opted to use the term scientific literacy.

Although educators and researchers from all disciplines have asserted that cultural, personal, and contextual factors influence a reader's approach and appropriation of a text (Barton and Hamilton; Perry, "Genres"; Purcell-Gates, *Other people's, Cultural; Street, Literacy, Social*), most research on scientific literacy stemming from science education and disciplinary literacy approaches has been carried out in one specific context—the school—and has traditionally looked at a particular type of involvement with the discipline—the "effective learning" of school science. Our study aims at contributing a richer view of what reading and writing about science mean for people with different social, cultural, and educational backgrounds. We looked at the roles that scientific literacy plays in the everyday lives of people outside the formal instruction environment by investigating the following research questions: 1) Do people read or write scientific content outside of the formal school context? 2) If so, what do the read and written texts look like? 3) What areas of people's lives are mediated by such texts? 4) What are people's purposes for reading and writing about science beyond the context of school?

In order to address these questions, we conducted a cross-case analysis of individual ethnographic case studies that investigated the literacy practices of members of various different marginalized communities around the world. With this study we uncover the nature of scientific literacy in its most fundamental sense (Norris and Phillips 226): the purposes and everyday life practices that contextualize people's reading and writing actions, with the goal of learning about science. In doing so, we advocate for a notion of scientific literacy that expands from school science to real-life engagement with science throughout society and by citizens of all ages, and we bring together two vibrant but independent fields of inquiry. We also contribute to addressing the need for novel empirical perspectives on scientific literacy research, which has been highlighted by Hand et al. as an essential element for bridging the gaps between literacy practices and the teaching and learning of science, and between research and policies (609).

Theoretical Framework

In general terms, science-education scholars agree that the science-education reforms that have taken place in Anglo countries within the past two decades promote standards-based definitions of scientific literacy for all learners (Yore, Bisanz, and Hand 690). For instance, scientific literacy has been outlined as knowledge or understanding of the content of science and its applications (DeBoer; Eisenhart, Finkel and Marion; NRC); ability to use scientific knowledge to solve problems (AAAS; NRC); understanding the nature of science (DeBoer; Hanrahan); or ability to think critically about science (Korpan et al.). Nonetheless, researchers from both the science-education and the disciplinary-literacy fields have contributed a more socially responsive perspective on scientific literacy that goes beyond the standards-based notions. Such views imply making the learning of science more accessible to youth and providing students/learners with access to functional and practical knowledge will allow them to evaluate ideas so they can make informed decisions or draw informed conclusions about the roles of science in their lives and those of others (Lemke; Moje; Norris and Phillips; Wellington and Osborne).

This last perspective on scientific literacy also brings into focus the specific roles that reading and writing have for science education and other disciplinary content areas—history, mathematics, English, etc. This body of work clearly considers that: a) literacy is not only the ability to read and write, but it is also a process that involves understanding and learning; b) both spoken and written language are integral parts of science and scientific literacy; and c) to be literate in any discipline, particular skills need to be developed (Moje; Norris and Phillips; Shanahan and Shanahan; Wellington and Osborne).

Norris and Phillips (225) differentiate between the fundamental sense of scientific literacy and its derived sense. According to them, the former refers to reading and writing when the content is science, or the practices surrounding the reading and writing of scientific written texts, and the latter refers to being knowledgeable, learned, and educated in science. Not many science-education scholars, Norris and Phillips argue, have contemplated the fundamental sense of scientific literacy as relevant for science and literacy education. In the disciplinary literacy field, however, researchers have made a strong argument that each discipline of knowledge demands particular ways of thinking, talking, reading, and writing and that those ways need to be taught in school through specific pedagogical strategies (Lemke; Moje; Shanahan and Shanahan). Scientific literacy in its fundamental sense then, also involves certain linguistic, cognitive, and cultural practices alongside the actual content matter of the text. In fact, a number of empirical studies have supported the conclusion that readers approach texts in different ways depending on their goals for reading them, the reader's involvement with the discipline in question, the nature and origins of the text itself, and the context in which the texts are being read (Moje 10).

Literacy and Scientific Literacy

Oral and written language is the symbol system most often used to do, teach, and learn about science, and the importance of language for scientific literacy has also been acknowledged (Hand et al. 608). Yet, the perceptions of the roles of language in science education, as well as the research approaches employed to investigate the roles of oral and written language in science teaching and learning, are constantly changing and have dramatically shifted over the last decades (Rudolph; Yore, Bisanz, and Hand). The initial focus on oral language as a source of speech and on the readability of textbooks eventually evolved—as a result of the development of the cognitive sciences and constructivist perspectives on learning—into an interest in the role of language in science and in science teaching and learning and the roles of learners' social and cultural context. Thus, in recent times we have seen an increasing awareness of the importance of the literacy component of scientific literacy, as well as of the social situated-ness of any learning event (Yore, Bisanz, and Hand 690). In fact, reading and writing research in science education has increased in the past two decades, although according to

Rudolph (66) and Yore, Bisanz, and Hand (691), most of it has been conducted in classroom settings with textbooks and worksheets as main focus points, and little has been done to explore the reading and writing of texts with scientific content in other contexts or the nature of the texts that are being read and written by people in order to gain new understandings around scientific topics and themes.

Studies concerned with the science education of a non-scientific public have been less common and diffused across a number of disciplines and fields (Rudolph 69). For the most part, such research has focused on the producers of the scientific texts, not on their readers and those readers' personal purposes and goals. For instance, Rudolph concluded that the main purposes of written texts geared for the general public are to explain the process of science, to foster scientific literacy, and to teach about the science of everyday things (70). Also, texts about science have been used in order to bring individuals from the non-scientific public, particularly underrepresented groups, closer to a meaningful relationship with science (74).

Disciplinary literacy, too, has seen a shift in perspective and focus through time. First, researchers focused on students' development of cognitive text processing strategies as a means of enhancing content-area learning without taking into consideration the specific demands of each discipline. Then more recently, disciplinary literacy moved to an approach that considers that learning disciplinary concepts takes place when students learn how knowledge is produced and consumed within the disciplines (Yore et al.). Other lines of current disciplinary literacy research focus on the particular roles of the linguistic processes of the disciplines and their implications for each content-area education (Halliday and Matthiessen). Disciplinary literacy researchers have also attempted to take the cultural practices and cognitive processes present in students' everyday lives into account and to draw from these in the process of creating novel subject-matter instructional tools (Barton; Moje; Roth and Lee). According to this perspective, content-area instruction should begin with students' interests, knowledge, and practice (Moje 5). Yet, this disciplinary literacy tradition has strongly focused on young students and their learning of the disciplines within the classroom setting; the greater part of the work done on connecting youth's culture and literacy practices to disciplinary knowledge, language and literacy comes from secondary English language arts and social studies (Moje 5).

Another branch of literacy research that has also employed a sociocultural lens has focused on the reading and writing of different written genres outside of school settings (Barton and Hamilton; Purcell-Gates, *Other people's, Cultural; Street, Literacy*). These researchers have viewed literacy as more than a collection of technical, acontextual skills, but rather as a tool that mediates people's lives and which reflects the social practices, history, and ongoing and shifting interactions that take place in the many contexts of people's daily lives.

There have also been numerous international calls to link language and scientific literacy with different audiences and language communities, stressing that multiple and varied language or literacy tasks could in fact increase both science understanding and language performance (Yore, Bisanz and Hand 691). In this regard, some research has been conducted in order to explore the reading and writing practices of scientists in their scientific inquiry endeavours (Berkenkotter and Huckin; Yore, Hand and Florence). However, few researchers have focused on exploring the nature of scientific genres amongst the lay people, and the purposes for using those genres, outside the context of formal instruction (Yore, Bisanz and Hand 693). Moreover, little has been done in the past to address communities that are socially, culturally, and economically marginalized from mainstream societies, and to explore the situations and contexts that influence their reading habits, strategies, and choices. Therefore, our research into scientific literacy outside of the classroom setting and into the everyday lives of culturally diverse people, framed by the view that scientific literacy exists in different forms, represents an important empirical contribution to both science education and disciplinary literacy.

The Cultural Practices of Literacy Study (CPLS). This research study, as part of the Cultural Practices of Literacy Study, is framed by theories that view literacy as always situated within social and cultural contexts and within relationships of power and ideology (Barton and Hamilton; Street, *Literacy*). Reading and writing, including reading and writing about science, is more than knowing words and locating information in a text. Many different elements contextualize and give meaning to any reading or writing event, such as the context where the event takes place, the characteristics of the text itself, the purpose for reading or writing, and the social and cultural backgrounds of people, as well as their linguistic and cognitive practices. Consequently, the analysis of any literacy practice is shaped by and interpreted within the sociocultural and sociolinguistic contexts within which it takes place (Barton and Hamilton; Bakhtin; Street, *Literacy, Social*; Vygotsky). This highlights the fact that texts are written and read for varied purposes and with varied meanings within specific sociocultural and sociolinguistic contexts. A pharmacist, for example, might read detailed chemical information about a new drug that has recently been developed, in order to be fully informed about the drug before dispensing it to patients, while a farmer might read the same text in order to make informed decisions and choices related to the use of the new product.

In this paper we identify and examine the scientific-literacy practices that have been reported by members of a collection of marginalized communities around the world. With this analysis, we explore what scientific literacy means to our participants in those social, cultural, linguistic, and economic contexts. We furthermore argue that investigating literacy practices in relation to science will provide a more realistic picture than now exists of the literacy and scientific worlds of students and their communities. At this time, what researchers know about scientific literacy and the lay public is limited and has not been a relevant focus of research. Researchers have acknowledged that we do not know much about people's appreciation or engagement with science, given the limited systematic inquiry in this field (Shapin 13). Our analysis offers a step towards filling this gap.

Method

The case studies from which the data for this analysis come represent a portion of the case studies that were conducted under the auspices of the Cultural Practices of Literacy Study. CPLS offers a theoretically grounded model to analyze and interpret accounts of literacy in context, and, for our purposes here, offers a unique approach to understanding scientific literacy across cultures and from the perspective of those who make use of written science genres (Purcell-Gates, Perry and Briseno).

The Cultural Practices of Literacy Study

Located at the University of British Columbia, CPLS is a large umbrella project focused on examining language and literacy practice in marginalized communities around the world (http://www.cpls.educ.ubc.ca/). Overlaying the Cultural Practices of Literacy Study is the primary focus on students and communities that have been historically marginalized in society and mainstream schools. CPLS consists of three main dimensions: (1) the collection of ethnographic case study data on the ways that literacy is practiced within specific cultural contexts; (2) the creation of an expanding database that allows for cross-case analyses of literacy practice (such as this one); and (3) the design of models of literacy instruction that reflect these data and that provide links between the literacy worlds of students and literacy instruction within formal educational contexts (Purcell-Gates, Perry and Briseno).

It must be stressed that CPLS researchers do not count frequencies or instances of a given text or event. Rather, we seek to capture an overview, or range, of the myriad practices available in a community, as well as the contexts that shape these practices for the participants of the study.

Currently, the Cultural Practices of Literacy Study includes a total of 24 individual case studies. All CPLS case studies focus on people engaging with print through literacy events within these contexts, and all of them contain data about the texts that mediate the sociocultural contexts within each case study and for each participant. Each CPLS case study examines literacy within sociocultural contexts and documents larger structures such as political, economic, historical, religious, linguistic, and power systems. In addition to describing literacy practices, each CPLS case study is also designed to answer its own specific research questions relevant to that particular sociocultural context. Although researchers pursue their own individual research questions, each researcher also collects data using a common methodology that allows the studies to contribute to the overall Cultural Practices of Literacy Study database and that allows for principled cross-case analyses.

The research study herein reported is one such CPLS cross-case analysis. With it, we begin to unveil: (a) the types of texts that are being read or written within particular sociocultural communities with the goal of learning about science, health and/or technology; (b) the purposes for which such texts are read and written; and (c) the domains of social activity in which such activities fall. Therefore, the present

CPLS cross-case analysis provides a much-needed exploration of the scientific-literacy practices that occur in people's everyday uses of language and literacy, with a particular focus on marginalized groups' perspectives. The present report is not, however, a frequency count of the number of scientific-literacy events, nor is it an analysis of the readers' interpretations of the contents of the texts or their impact in people's scientific understanding. Rather, we provide an exploratory overview of the landscape of scientific literacy amongst marginalized people around the world.

Data Collection for Cultural Practices of Literacy Study

All Cultural Practices of Literacy Study case studies are organized around a common methodology for data collection and data analysis, which allows us to conduct principled analyses across multiple cases. Common CPLS data sources include: (a) field and participant observation of the ways that people engage with print, and of the social, cultural, and political contexts within which such events occur; (b) semi-structured interviews with participants; (c) documentation of 'public texts' (through photographs or collection of artifacts) such as texts found in stores, advertisements on bus stops, newspapers, and so on. For a detailed description on the data collection and data analysis methods and schemes used in CPLS, see Purcell-Gates, Perry, and Briseno and http://www.cpls.educ.ubc.ca.

Again, CPLS researchers do not aim to document the frequency of people's reading and writing events. Also, CPLS is not specifically focused in scientific literacy but in documenting the wide range of literacy practices of the members of the communities under analysis, which may include scientific literacy. For example, science-related literacy events often emerged as casual or spontaneous comments made by participants about the things that they regularly read and/or write in their daily lives.

Coding System for the CPLS Studies

Our common coding system permits researchers to systematically analyze data from individual case studies in ways that reflect the theories of literacy as socially situated, socially semiotic, multiple, and mediating social lives. All literacy practice data from the Cultural Practices of Literacy Study case studies are coded at the literacy event level. Following Shirley Brice Heath, we define "literacy event" as any observable or reported instance of reading and writing. Our codes include theoretically-based codes (e.g. social activity domain; text type; purpose; and function), as well as descriptive codes (e.g. mode of literacy engagement: reading, writing, listening to; language(s) of the text; or whether the event occurred in participant's childhood or adulthood) and demographic codes (e.g. participant's age, gender, occupation(s), country of birth, native language(s), language(s) spoken at home, language(s) read or written, level of schooling completed, etc). Codes that are relevant to this analysis are included in Table 1.

Table 1: CPLS codes containing relevant information for the cross-case analysis on scientific literacy

Code	Definition
Domain of social activity (Dm)	Reflects a focused area of common activity engaged in by people that can be named and recognized as shaping textual activity, social relationships, roles, purposes, aims, and social expectations. Examples are entertaining oneself or having fun; participating in family life; attending to health and hygiene; participating in formal schooling; and working.
Function (Fn)	Is what happens in order to achieve a given comprehension or expressive purpose. A literacy event's function is implied by the text. A function drives the intent of reading/writing.
Social Purpose (Pr)	Is the ultimate goal of the literacy event within a particular social activity domain. The social purpose is implied by the domain, as opposed to the function which is implied by the text itself. For example, in the domain of working, the purpose of writing a resume is to apply for (and perhaps) receive a job.
Text type (Tx)	Genre of the text involved in any literacy practice, as defined by purpose of the text and relevant textual features. The materiality or form of the text (e.g., book, magazine, notebook, and digital forms) is also included in this code.
Mode (Md)	Type of literacy activity: reading or writing.
Language (Lg)	The language of the text involved in the literacy event.
Demographic data	Age, gender, spoken languages, level of schooling, occupation, access to computers and internet, etc.

Source: Purcell-Gates, Perry and Briseno.

The CPLS coding system provides a consistent, theoretical way of linking individual literacy events to a larger set of contextual data, such as interview transcripts or field notes. Each study with its codes, along with its corresponding field notes, photos, artifacts, and published and unpublished reports, is loaded into an electronic and searchable database. The large CPLS database allows researchers to perform queries according to particular research interests, and to go back to the original field notes and interpretations.

Data Collection for Cross-Case Analysis: Selection of Cases for Analysis

To identify instances of scientific literacy in the database, we began by exploring our list of functions for reading or writing "Fn". The Fn code captures the immediate communicative intent of a reading or writing event and is directly connected to the nature of the text and from the perspective of the participant. The Cultural Practices of Literacy Study database includes instances of function codes such as "To learn about science", "To learn about plants/gardening", and "To learn about human physiology". All original Fn codes that refer to science, animals/plants, health/physiology, technology, and psychology were included in this initial phase of case selection. Following this line of reasoning, we argue that any text genre that from a participant's perspective is used with the goal of learning about science, health, and/or technology ought to be identified as a crucial component of that person's scientific-literacy practices.

We deliberately chose to include health and technology in this analysis of scientific literacy because we consider these knowledge areas to be closely related to the current scientific endeavour as well as components of the science curriculum for elementary, middle, and high school students around the world. On the other hand, we also chose to leave any activities that relate to participating in formal schooling out of this analysis, because we were particularly interested in providing readers with a fuller and clearer picture of non-school related scientific-literacy events. For instance, the many reported instances of parents/guardians helping children with school related activities were not taken into consideration for this analysis.

Generic Fn codes such as "To learn about interesting things", "To compose essay", "To record notes from reading", and "To summarize information" were also investigated. After identifying the relevant Fn codes, we returned to the database to more closely examine the contextual data from field notes, transcripts, and researchers' interpretations and reports. By this means we were able to: a) corroborate which literacy events were actually related to learning about science, health and/or technology and b) give context and meaning to the selected literacy events. Analyzing literacy practices data in conjunction with the overall contextual data for each study is an essential step in any CPLS cross-case analysis, as this provides a grounded perspective of the contextual factors that surround each of the selected codes and literacy events. In other words, the literacy event data cannot stand on their own and must be analyzed and understood within the sociocultural contexts in which they occur. After identifying the relevant literacy events along with their corresponding case studies—as described below— we queried the large electronic database to pinpoint information that we considered pertinent for the objectives of the present cross-case analysis, including domain of social activity, purpose for reading or writing, text type, mode, and language (Table 1). We also identified relevant demographic data.

Cases Included in this Analysis

From the database, we identified numerous reading and writing events that had learning about science, health, and/or technology as a goal. These events were represented in 19 of the 24 case studies that currently comprise the CPLS database. Altogether, these 19 case studies represent diverse social and cultural communities worldwide (Table 2). Our findings speak to the fact that scientific-literacy activities are represented among the real-world literacy practices of a wide variety of marginalized participants and communities.

Table 2: Individual CPLS case studies included in the cross-case analysis on scientific literacy

Case No.	Description
Case 1	Ecology of reading and writing and the everyday lives of the inmates at the state prison in Oaxaca, Mexico (Clemente and Higgins).
Case 2	Literacy practices of a group of elementary school students living in a shelter in Oaxaca, Mexico (Clemente and Higgins).
Case 3	Literacy practices of future English teachers currently enrolled in a university teacher education program in Oaxaca, Mexico (Clemente and Higgins).
Case 4	Attitudes toward and usage of English among two farmers in Puerto Rico (Mazak, "Appropriation").
Case 5	Usages of English in a rural, Puerto Rican community (Mazak, "Negotiating").
Case 6	Literacy practices of several families living in a marginalized, mainly non-English L1 neighborhood of urban Vancouver, Canada (CPLS).
Case 7	How a U.S. course in writing and technology helps university students acquire a technology discourse and reflect critically upon digital literacy practices (Eyman).
Case 8	Literacy activities, beliefs and values of two Chinese-American bilingual families (Zhang).
Case 9	Changes of one family's literacy practices brought about by life changes after immigrating from Korea to Canada (Kim).
Case 10	Home and school literacy practices of a group of fifth grade, urban students attending an after-school program in the U.S. (Kersten).
Case 11	Literacy practices of three male Sudanese refugee youth living in Michigan, U.S. (Perry, "Sharing").
Case 12	Literacy practices of Sudanese families with young children living in the U.S., focusing on literacy brokering (Perry, "Genres").

Case 13	Elementary students' literacy practices in L2 (Spanish) and emergence into Spanish literacy as L1 Zapoteco speakers in Mexico (Velasco-Zárate).
Case 14	Literacy practices of two adult Cuban refugees in the U.S. (Rosolová).
Case 15	Literacy practices of parents with no or low schooling, who have moved from rural to urban areas to provide greater educational opportunities for their children in Oaxaca, Mexico (López).
Case 16	Literacy practices in an East Vancouver (Canada) neighborhood whose elementary school ranks in the lowest quartile of British Columbia schools (Moayeri and Smith).
Case 17	Literacy practices of students in a Bolivian Fe y Alegria School, teachers' preparation to teach in culturally responsive ways (Gates and Purcell-Gates).
Case 18	Literacy practices of L1 Spanish migrant farm worker families in the US, and their children's literacy experiences attending English Head Start programs (Purcell-Gates, "Literacy practices").
Case 19	Relationship between the in- and out-of-school literacy practices of marginalized Nicaraguan immigrant students in Costa Rica (Purcell-Gates, "Cultural").

Demographic Characteristics of Participants

This cross-case analysis reports on the data from approximately 380 participants. Some of these 380 individuals were focal participants in their case studies, while others were non-focal participants (e.g., relatives or community members whose literacy practices may have been described by focal participants or who may have been observed by the researcher but not directly interviewed). Participants from the different social and cultural communities in the cases described above included children, youths, young adults, adults, and seniors ranging in age from 5 to 70 years old. Females and males were fully represented in our database, although the female population for this particular analysis was slightly larger.

This analysis included individuals with differing levels of schooling completed. Participants ranged from having no schooling whatsoever to participants with doctoral degrees; all levels of schooling completed in between were represented (e.g. some elementary/primary school, some high school, and some college, and master's degrees). It is interesting to note that over 40% of participants of this cross-case analysis only completed some elementary school or had no formal education at all. Approximately one half the participants who had no formal schooling or only some elementary schooling were children under the age of 12; their levels of schooling therefore compare to their ages. The remaining half, however, corresponds to young adults and adults between 13 to 70 years of age. This indicates that, according to our data, adults with limited formal education were reading and writing to, from their perspective, learn about science in their everyday lives. Close to 15% of participants had completed some college, and another 15% held a college degree. Only about 6% of participants had attained graduate degrees.

Participants' occupations also represented a rich range of activities, including: actor, baker, business owner, carpenter, child care provider, construction worker, doctor, domestic help, electrician, factory worker, fisherman, government employee, housewife/homemaker, migrant farm worker, school principal, secretary, shoemaker, store clerk, student, subsistence farmer, teacher, and no occupation.

The pool of people included in this cross-case analysis represented a rich variety of first or home languages including: Aymara, Baria, Chatino, Chontal, Cree, Konkani, Latuka, Nuba, Tlingit, Triqui, Vietnamese, West Indian Patois, Zande, and Zoque. However, literacy and literacy instruction in these communities took place primarily in the following languages: Arabic, Dinka, English, French, Greek, Hindi, Ilocano, KiSwahili, Korean, Madi, Mandarin, Marathi, Mixe, Punjabi, Quechua, Spanish, Tagalog, Tamil, Vietnamese, and Zapoteco.

The communities included in this research study were diverse and unique, but shared the common characteristic of a marginalized status within their respective socio-political communities. The groups of people herein included were comprised of immigrants (both legal and illegal), refugees, citizens, and legal work/study visa holders. Nearly 50% of participants lived in urban settings, while almost 30% resided in rural areas; around 20% lived in suburban settings, and a small percentage dwelled in small towns. Less than 30% of the participants had computers in their homes, and only 15% had access to the Internet through home connections. However, almost all participants had Internet access near their homes—a fact that had a direct impact on their access to texts used to learn about science.

In the findings section, we will describe and elaborate on the nature of the reading and writing events that can be catalogued as components of the scientific-literacy practices of the participants and their communities.

Findings and Discussion

Our analysis indicates that participants read and wrote about science as part of different activities that were not related to school endeavours. Such literacy events took place in many different spheres of people's lives and involved a diverse range of text types that were read or written for varied social purposes.

Scientific Literacy across Different Domains of Human Activity

Science reading events largely exceeded science writing events, and the reading events were engaged in for a wider range of social domains. Science reading was done within the following social activity domains: Entertaining oneself, having fun "ENT"; participating in family life "FAM"; attending to health and hygiene "HTH"; acquiring or disseminating information/news "INF"; maintaining tools and home environment

"MTN"; transacting with school-like learning practices "SLL"; engaging in self-motivated education/personal improvement "SME"; and working "WRK". Science writing, on the other hand, was reported or observed within the following social activity domains: ENT; FAM; HTH; INF; SME; and WRK. These outcomes accord with other studies of literacy practice that document a higher incidence of reported reading than writing events (e.g., Purcell-Gates et al). As will be fully discussed, our findings, give a sense of the everyday scientific-literacy events for participants and communities from participants' perspective.

Of course, many of the reported reading and writing events related to science had a connection with formal instruction or schooling, and took place as a result of people's direct involvement with science learning at school. These instances are not, however, discussed in this paper.

Our analysis offers rich evidence that varied scientific-literacy events occurred outside of formal schooling. Non-educated as well as educated people, as part of their everyday lives, read and wrote about science as part of their leisure activities, as a source of information about current events, as a means of attending to their own health, and as a result of a self-motivated interest in learning and improving their understanding of the natural world. Examples of reported scientific-literacy events include a prisoner in Oaxaca, Mexico reading a science article in a magazine in order to pass time; a Bolivian mother writing an informative summary about a reading on diverse topics, including science, in order to explain information to her child; a Mexican immigrant farmer in the U.S. reading information books about pregnancy and child diets in order to keep her family and herself healthy; a child in a shelter reading a textbook about geography in order to make sense of the news in the newspaper; a low-educated Oaxacan parent reading about plants and gardening in order to learn something new; two young Sudanese refugees in the U.S. reading a children's picture dictionary to learn about animals and satisfy curiosity; a farmer in Puerto Rico learning information about animal health in order to meet job requirements; and a Vancouver resident of an immigrant neighbourhood reading about technology in order to be able to fix computers. In this particular case, the woman explained to the researcher that although she is not an educated person, she is now capable of using a computer, installing programs, and actually fixing and putting together machines from parts—results of her own interest and reading practices:

> **Participant:** Yeah. Well I read a lot of stuff on like, I'm getting really good at the computer. I do all my own thing on it. Like I've learned from ... well I didn't go to school, I just did it on my own.
>
> *Researcher:* Like figuring out the word processing and that kind of stuff?
>
> **Participant:** Yeah. And how to fix it, take it apart.
>
> *Researcher:* Oh really?
>
> **Participant:** I take them all apart.
>
> *Researcher:* You can take like the hard drive?

Participant: I like taking things apart ... When I bought my first computer I got the screwdriver out and I took it all apart.

Researcher: Oh really? I would be terrified.

Participant: I add memory, I do all sorts of things, clean them.

An interesting finding is that in fact, many of the reported reading events that had learning about science, health, and technology as a goal, fell within the domains of entertainment and self-motivated education. The fact that participants engaged in science-learning practices out of the school setting moved by personal motives suggests that such scientific-literacy events could impact people's appreciation and understanding of science beyond the aims and scope of formal schooling. This outcome, then, challenges the widespread interest in school science as the only avenue for science education and raises questions about the actual significance of investigating and valuing students' everyday worlds.

Table 3: Purposes for engaging in reading events, outside the domain of schooling, that have learning about science, health and/or technology as a goal

In order to alleviate depression/stress/loneliness	In order to learn/improve skills in another language
In order to apply for/get a job	In order to meet job requirements
In order to be correctly informed	In order to monitor child's learning/achievement
In order to be entertained	
In order to be informed about events/issues	In order to pass time
	In order to relax
In order to educate oneself	In order to satisfy curiosity
In order to improve one self	In order to share text/information with someone
In order to keep self/family healthy	
In order to know if one needs medical care	In order to understand content
In order to learn new things/skills	In order to understand instructions
In order to learn/improve literacy skills	In order to use a computer

Social Purposes for Reading/Writing to Learn About Science

We expect social purposes and domains of social activity to be intimately related, since according to our model of literacy practice (Purcell-Gates, Perry and Briseno), the social purpose or reason for any reading or writing to be done is implied by the domain of social activity in which the literacy event takes place. However, an exploration of the social purposes for reading or writing about science provides a more clear and detailed picture of the objectives attained by the members of the communities included in this analysis, when engaging in the aforementioned literacy events beyond the domain of formal schooling. The social purposes related to reading about science are outlined in Table 4, and Table 5 shows the social purposes related to writing about science beyond the formal schooling context.

Table 4: Purposes for engaging in writing events, outside the domain of schooling, that have learning about science, health and/or technology as a goal

In order to be entertained	In order to play/do/solve game/puzzle/activity
In order to get website information	
In order to keep self/family healthy	In order to remember events/dates/information
In order to learn new things/skills	
In order to learn/improve skills in another language	In order to share text/information with someone
In order to pass time	In order to understand content

Table 5: Text genres read and/or written by the participants of the different CPLS studies, with the goal of learning about science

	Case 1	Case 2	Case 3	Case 4	Case 5	Case 6	Case 7	Case 8
Advertisement								
Almanac								
Caption								
Copy text								
Dictionary								
Encyclopedia entry	R							
Encyclopedia set	R							
Essay			W					
Feature story								
Fiction narrative			R	R				
Information note		W		W		W	W	W
Information text	R/W		R/W	R	R	R/W		
Instructional text	R	R	R	R	R	R	R	R/W
Instructions								
Manual								
News story				R				
Novel								
Product catalogue						R		
Reading notes			W					
Research report						R	R	
Search term			W					W
Self-help text						R		
Sentence		W						
Table of contents				R				

Case 9	Case 10	Case 11	Case 12	Case 13	Case 14	Case 15	Case 16	Case 17	Case 18	Case 19
				R						R
								R		
	R									
			W							
			R			R				
						R		R		
				R						
				W						
							R			R
			W	W						
	R	R	R	R/W	R	R/W	R/W	R/W	R	R
	R	R	R	R		R	R	R	R	
								R		
							R			
				R		R		R	R	
								R		
				W						
							R			
W										
				R						

Social purposes for reading about science. Some examples from the data include: a farmer in Puerto Rico reading a news story related to science "in order to relax"; an East Vancouver parent reading about technology "in order to share text/information with someone", in this case his children; an East Vancouver mother reading pamphlets about health "in order to be informed about events/issues"; a Zapoteco native reading a science encyclopedia "in order to learn new things/skills"; a Puerto Rican farmer reading health handbooks "in order to meet job requirements"; and, as illustrated in the following quote, a Nicaraguan immigrant in Costa Rica reading magazine articles about medicine and health "in order to keep self/family healthy":

> **Participant:** In these "Selecciones" magazines, there is always a section on medicine. The one I am reading now talks about how to floss your teeth. It talks about dental hygiene. It talks about cavities and how they are formed. All of that. The issue I am reading now has all that information. Dental care. I have it here ... It exactly talks about those things, about health care, I mean personal hygiene and dental care ... Here. I have read up to this page ... It also talks about obesity and how to prevent obesity in children ... See? It talks about nutrition and what the children need, and has a nutrition pyramid.

Social purposes for writing about science. Some examples of writing events include: members of bilingual Chinese American families creating instructional materials "in order to teach a lesson" on geometry and astronomy; a Korean mother in Vancouver typing search terms in a browser "in order to get website information" about health issues; and a future English teacher in Oaxaca, Mexico, taking notes in English from reading information text about interesting facts in nature "in order to learn/improve skills in another language". The following quote exemplifies this last event:

> **Participant:** I like reading about many things, like nature and also politics, and entertainment too. We have many books at home. But I also like to write down about the things I found most interesting ... So that is what I do during the day ...
>
> *Researcher:* You don't do it in Spanish?
>
> **Participant:** No
>
> *Researcher:* Because you want to practice your English.
>
> **Participant:** Right, my English.

The individual case studies included in this analysis take account of diverse communities with varied social and cultural realities. For many of the communities represented by the participants of these case studies, life involves a daily struggle to survive within circumstances that constantly shape their daily activities and their perceptions of the world. In these contexts, scientific literacy seems to take a different meaning from that traditionally stressed by researchers and authorities (e.g. AAAS; NRC). Even when "comprehending and appreciating the nature of science" or "acquiring and using logical arguments and plausible reasoning in order to explain patterns in the natural world" might not be relevant goals for these communities, we argue that their engagement with texts and the social purposes for which they read or write about science ought to be considered as one of the many forms of scientific literacy. As DeBoer states, "There are many ways to be scientifically literate" (597).

Texts that Participants Read and Wrote "To Learn about Science"

An exploration of the texts that were reported or observed as being read or written to learn about science across the individual case studies included in this analysis revealed the text types that were accessible, meaningful, and relevant for the communities under analysis beyond attending to formal schooling-related activities. Interestingly, our analysis indicates that although writing about science took place in fewer different domains of social activity than reading about science, we were able to identify an equally diverse arrangement of text types or genres associated with writing (Table 5).

The literary practice of reading and writing about science was part of different activities in our participants' everyday lives. Among the genres associated with reading events, information and instructional texts constitute a substantial portion of the total arrangement of reported or observed read text types, and these genres are also well represented amongst the reported writing events. *Information text* refers to print that provides content or factual knowledge for someone who does not have it and wants or needs it. It is expository text that is used outside the context of an instructional setting or activity. *Instructional text*, on the other hand, also conveys information for someone who does not have it, but it is meant to instruct or educate people on some topic, on how to do something, or to facilitate learning a particular skill. It is used within some sort of instructional setting, like school or the workplace, or at home when instruction/education is involved. This means that even though there was not a vast diversity in the reported read or written genres in relation to science, there were many reports of people reading and writing instructional text –e.g., textbooks, for their own personal purposes of learning about science, and not because the schooling context led them to such actions.

The different genres associated with scientific literacy were represented in several different physical forms, such as books, newspapers, websites, magazines, textbooks, pamphlets, and scholarly journals. Moreover, the presence of digital forms of text such as e-encyclopaedias, e-journals, reference websites, and electronic documents in general is to be acknowledged, considering the low incidence of computers in the homes of participants.

According to Yore, Bisanz and Hand (693), different text genres have been identified and associated with the doing of science, ranging from interpersonal communication notes to scientific journal papers. Other genres that aim at communicating scientific issues or content to the layperson, in the form of newspapers or magazines, have also been pointed out by researchers as elements for scientific literacy. But what has traditionally interested researchers and educators is the role of textbooks in scientific literacy (Rudolph; Yore, Bisanz and Hand).

Our examination of the literacy practices of different cultural communities shows that the elements of scientific literacy are not a uniform set of documents, but they comprise more than journal papers, newspaper articles, and traditional textbooks. Such diversity of genres associated with scientific literacy can be differentiated according to the social and cultural purposes they achieve in society –e.g., texts that popularize information generated in the scientific community. Our findings show that diverse genres intended to popularize science, such as news stories and information text in the form of books, magazines, or websites, are being utilized by people as part of their cultural practices of scientific literacy. According to Yore, Bisanz and Hand (705), reports about scientific and medical research are commonly found in the media, including the Internet, and our study corroborates this assertion.

Moreover, the presence of information texts in the form of scholarly journals merits some particular consideration given the attention that this specific genre has received from education researchers in the past decades. Scholarly journals have been deemed the pinnacle of scientific work, the primary product of scientists, and one of the most used forms of print amongst scientists (Yore, Bisanz and Hand 695). Our analysis indicates that the members of the communities represented in this study read these texts as part of activities outside formal schooling, and that such activities fell within the domains of health, self-motivated education, and work. For instance, an East Vancouver resident for whom English is not her first language read a journal article to learn new information that would help her carry out her job requirements; a university student in the U.S. read an article about information technology driven by his own interests to learn new information; and an immigrant in Vancouver read a journal article on medicine with the purpose of taking care of his own health.

Some researchers have raised the question as to the influence of language and culture on science understanding and interpretations –e.g., Sutherland and Dennick. Although it is our belief that culture may in fact influence the type of knowledge constructed about nature and the outside world, and that any formal instruction should take place in the language used by learners, such discussions are beyond the scope of our analysis. However, what is relevant for this study is the fact that scientific-literacy practices actually reflect the multicultural realities of our participants. In fact, Arabic, English, French, Hindi, Punjabi, Sinhalese, Spanish, and Tamil were the languages of the texts read and written by the participants of the individual case studies included in this analysis. Also, we assert that cultural contexts determine to a greater extent the nature of people's scientific-literacy practices. For instance, a farmer in Puerto Rico is interested in the health of her children, whereas a prisoner in Oaxaca finds ways of escaping reality and alleviating stress and depression by learning about science and technology. Or Zapoteco children in Oaxaca who have Spanish as a second language are interested in learning new things and skills, whereas a Cuban immigrant in the U.S. is interested in learning about forensics driven by a personal interest and as a means for entertaining herself.

Conclusions

Scientific-literacy research offers a chance to understand science in sociocultural contexts outside of school. This analysis of scientific literacy contributes to a better and richer understanding of how science and the community members interact on an everyday basis. In this paper, we presented an analysis of literacy-practice data collected over several years in multiple cultural and social communities around the globe. With this effort, we address an area of inquiry that has been traditionally overlooked by researchers and education personnel: scientific literacy as cultural practice in marginalized communities.

Experts have highlighted that some of the goals of scientific literacy ought to be the productive participation of society in scientific practices and discourse, the making of political, community, and personal decisions based on scientific knowledge, and so on. However, it is our view that the relevance of scientific literacy ought to reside in its potential to enable people to find solutions to their everyday problems and personal questions. In its most basic and fundamental sense, scientific literacy should not be solely about economic returns or the evaluation of scientific evidence and explanations. It should not be about only understanding the nature of science or becoming scientifically proficient. It should also be about empowering people to use scientific knowledge to support their everyday efforts at living a full and satisfying life.

Our analysis does not focus on traditional notions of scientific literacy and scientific proficiency. Rather, it addresses scientific literacy in its fundamental sense (Norris and Phillips 226). It illustrates that texts read and written to learn about science play several different roles in the ordinary lives of ordinary people. Our analysis also uncovers real-life scientific-literacy events and their relevance for the layperson and their communities. Our analysis of scientific literacy reveals community members engaging in scientific reading and writing for a wide array of social purposes and within an array of social activity domains – all indicators that scientific literacy is actively practiced within different sociocultural communities. Further, this activity is present within groups that are marginalized politically, socially, and linguistically – something that may be surprising to many teachers. The outcomes of this study challenge the somewhat widespread perception that many people do not read or write beyond the school context with the genuine goal of learning about science and supports the claim that people have a very active role in their scientific literacy-related activities.

Bearing in mind that this cross-case analysis is based on literacy-as-cultural-practice data that does not have scientific literacy as a main focus of research, the outcomes we present here have significant implications for science education and science-education research. Firstly, the findings of this study acknowledge that scientific literacy, understood as reading and writing with the objective of learning about science, is an element of the quotidian literacy practices of people and that scientific-literacy events occur naturally beyond the formal schooling context and in interconnectedness to people's diverse activities. Secondly, as Stephen Norris and Linda Phillips suggest, science-instruction endeavours ought to include teachers' integrated use and understanding of print and everyday scientific literacy practices and not just the teaching of scientific facts and theories. Teacher awareness of students' outside worlds is crucial to finding effective ways to build on the prior knowledge and experiences students bring to the classroom setting. This study represents an effort to describe the nature of the literacy practices that people from specific communities around the world consider as supporting their learning about science, health, and/or technology and therefore contributes to our understanding about what students are engaged in outside of school. As Elizabeth Moje claims, educators who can hear, understand, respect, and incorporate what students bring to the classroom are able to build on those everyday practices as resources for bridging and supporting student learning across disciplines. Finally, although the focus of this study is promising in terms of providing a grounded overview of the nature of the literacy practices that people engage in with the goal of learning about science, more research is needed in order to be able to make informed recommendations for formal science instruction. For instance, research specifically focused on the scientific-literacy practices of particular communities in particular contexts, would be useful in order to discern in detail the ways in which people interact with particular texts, the tasks they face, and the ways in which they deal with new or conflicting concepts and ultimately build on their understandings and explanations around scientific topics and issues.

Currently, explanation and argumentation are seen as crucial elements in science, science discourse, and science education (Hammer, Russ, Mikeska, and Scherr; Krajcik and Sutherland; Lemke). Research that explores how people from marginalized communities build on their real-world scientific knowledge and literacy practices in order to craft explanations and arguments around scientific topics also represents an avenue of important contributions to the field of science education. Understanding students' customary ways of structuring explanations could inform real-life instruction around canonic scientific explanation and argumentation practices.

Formal science instruction can help prepare students to engage meaningfully with the natural world only when students' real worlds are acknowledged and activities inspired by real life are implemented. To accomplish this, science education could involve instruction on the interpretation of the different types of texts and text forms that are part of science, the different domains of everyday life where science is relevant, and how all of this interrelates in the world outside of school. In doing so, the literacy worlds of students inevitably will be recognized and built upon in the formal instructional context.

One of the objectives of CLPS is to draw on real-life literacy practices in order to inform models of literacy instruction in ways that are relevant and motivating for learners. Relevance, as Miia Rannikmäe, Moonika Teppo, and Jack Holbrook assert (117), is established when learners are able to see how the received instruction relates to their customary realities. This analysis, by means of exploring the nature of learners' real-life scientific-literacy practices, represents a step forward towards a science-education model that helps learners recognise that science has relevance for their current and future lives.

In this analysis we have given voice to several minorities who are commonly excluded from the discussions around scientific literacy and what it should entail. Scientific literacy, in our view, is not a commodity that can be acquired, but a lifelong practice with real-world ends. It is always contextualized and meaningful when related to the specific needs and realities of people. Reconceptualising scientific literacy will expand the notion of science education from being solely a school-based endeavour to include all the activities that take place both inside and outside schools and the cultural and social elements that shape them.

Works Cited

American Association for the Advancement of Science. *Benchmarks for Science Literacy*. Washington, D.C.: AAAS, 1993. Print.

Askehave, Inger and John Malcolm Swales. "Genre Identification and Communicative Purpose: A Problem and a Possible Solution." *Applied Linguistics* 22.2 (2001): 195-212. Print.

Bakhtin, Mikhail M. *Speech Genres & Other Late Essays*. Austin: University of Texas Press, 1986. Print.

Barton, David and Mary Hamilton. *Local Literacies: Reading and Writing in One Community*. London: Routledge, 1998. Print.

Berkenkotter, Carol and Thomas N. Huckin. *Genre Knowledge in Disciplinary Communication: Cognition/Culture/Power*. Hillsdale, NJ: Erlbaum, 1995. Print.

Clemente, Ángeles and Michael Higgins. "Moving Between Imagined Communities of Literacy." *Cultural Practices of Literacy Study*. N.p., n.d. Web. 6 Mar. 2012.

Cultural Practices of Literacy Study."Vancouver Case Studies of Underachieving School Communities."*Cultural Practices of Literacy Study*. N.p., n.d. Web. 6Mar.2012.

DeBoer, George E. "Scientific Literacy: Another Look at its Historical and Contemporary Meanings and its Relationship to Science Education Reform." *Journal of Research in Science Teaching* 37 (2000): 582–601. Print.

Eisenhart, Margaret, Elizabeth Finkel, and Scott F. Marion. "Creating the Conditions for Scientific Literacy: A Re-examination." American Educational Research Journal 33 (1996): 261–295. *JSTOR Arts & Sciences IV Archive Collection*. Web. 20 Feb. 2012.

Eyman, Douglas. "Digital Literac(ies), Digital Discourses, and Communities of Practice: Literacy Practices in Virtual Environments." *Cultural Practices of Literacy: Case Studies of Language, Literacy, Social Practice, and Power*. Ed. Victoria Purcell-Gates. Mahwah, NJ: Lawrence Erlbaum, 2007. 181-195. Print.

Feinstein, Noah. "Salvaging Science Literacy." *Science Education* 95 (2011): 168–185. Print.

Freedman, Aviva and Peter Medway. *Genre and the New Rhetoric*. London: Taylor & Francis: 1994. Print.

Gates, Tracy and Victoria Purcell-Gates. "Culturally responsive literacy instruction: A case study of a Fe y Alegria school in Bolivia." *Cultural Practices of Literacy Study*. N.p., n.d. Web. 6 Mar. 2012.

Halliday, Michael Alexander K. and Christian M. Matthiessen, M. *An Introduction to Functional Grammar.* London: Arnold, 2004. Print.

Hand, Brian M., Donna E. Alvermann, James Gee, Barbara J. Guzzetti, Stephen P. Norris, Linda M. Phillips, Vaughan Prain, and Larry D. Yore. "Message from the "Island group": What is Literacy in Science Literacy?." *Journal of Research in Science Teaching* 40 (2003): 607–615. Print.

Hanrahan, Mary. "Rethinking Science Literacy: Enhancing Communication and Participation in School Science through Affirmational Dialogue Journal Writing." *Journal of Research in Science Teaching* 36 (1999): 699–717. *Wiley Online Library.* Web. 20 Feb. 2012.

Heath, Shirley Brice. "Protean Shapes in Literacy Events: Ever-Shifting Oral and Literate Traditions." *Spoken and Written Language: Exploring Orality and Literacy.* Ed. Deborah Tannen. Norwood, NJ: Ablex, 1982. 91-117. Print.

Hammer, David, Rosemary Russ, Jamie Mikeska, and Rachel Scherr. "Identifying Inquiry and Conceptualizing Students' Abilities." *Establishing a Consensus Agenda for K-12 Science Inquiry.* Ed. Richard Duschl and Richard Grandy. Rotterdam, NL: Sense Publishers, 2008. Print.

Kersten, Jodene. "Literacy and Choice: Urban Elementary Students' Perceptions of Links between Home, School, and Community Literacy Practices." *Cultural Practices of Literacy: Case Studies of Language, Literacy, Social Practice, and Power.* Ed. Victoria Purcell-Gates. Mahwah, NJ: Lawrence Erlbaum, 2007. 133-154. Print.

Kim, Ji-Eun. (n.d.). "New Life Style Brings New Literacy Practices for a Korean Immigrant Family in Canada." *Cultural Practices of Literacy Study.* N.p., n.d. Web. 6 Mar. 2012.

Korpan, Connie, A. Gay L. Bisanz, Jeffrey Bisanz, and John M. Henderson. "Assessing Literacy in Science: Evaluation of Scientific News Briefs." *Science Education* 81 (1997): 515–532. Print.

Krajcik, Joseph S. and LeeAnn M. Sutherland. "Supporting Students in Developing Literacy in Science." *Science* 328.5977 (2010): 456-459. *Science Magazine.* Web. 20 Feb. 2012.

Lemke, Jay L. *Talking Science: Language, Learning, and Values.* Norwood, NJ: Ablex, 1990. Print.

López, Mario. "Cultural Literacy Practices and Imagined Futures of Parents with No or Low Levels of Formal Schooling: Parents and Children's Perspectives." *Cultural Practices of Literacy Study.* N.p., n.d. Web. 6 Mar. 2012.

Mazak, Catherine M. "Appropriation and Resistance in the (English) Literacy Practices of Puerto Rican Farmers." *Cultural Practices of Literacy: Case Studies of Language, Literacy, Social Practice, and Power.* Ed. Victoria Purcell-Gates. Mahwah, NJ: Lawrence Erlbaum, 2007. 25-40. Print.

_____. "Negotiating el Difícil: Uses of English Text in a Rural Puerto Rican Community." *Centro Journal* 20.1 (2008): 50-71. Print.

Moayeri, Maryam and Jane Smith. "The Unfinished Stories of Two First Nations Mothers." *Journal of Adolescent & Adult Literacy* 53.5 (2010): 408-417. *Education Research Complete*. Web. 22 Feb. 2012.

Moje, Elizabeth Birr. "Developing Socially Just Subject-Matter Instruction: A Review of the Literature on Disciplinary Literacy Teaching." *Review of Research in Education* 31 (2007): 1-44. *SAGE Journals Online Archive*. Web. 20 Feb. 2012.

National Research Council. *National Science Education Standards*. Washington, D.C.: National Academy of Sciences, 1996. Print.

Norris, Stephen P. and Linda M. Phillips. "How Literacy in its Fundamental Sense is Central to Scientific Literacy." *Science Education* 87 (2003): 224-240. Print.

Perry, Kristen. "Sharing Stories, Linking Lives: Literacy Practices among Sudanese Refugees." *Cultural Practices of Literacy: Case Studies of Language, Literacy, Social Practice, and Power*. Ed. Victoria Purcell-Gates. Mahwah, NJ: Lawrence Erlbaum, 2007. 57-84. Print.

———. "Genres, Contexts, and Literacy Practices: Literacy Brokering among Sudanese Refugee Families." *Reading Research Quarterly* 44.3 (2009): 256-276. Print.

Purcell-Gates, Victoria. "Literacy Practices of U.S. Migrant Workers with Young Children in Head Start." *Cultural Practices of Literacy Study*. N.p., n.d. Web. 6 Mar. 2012.

———. "Cultural Practices of Literacy: A case of Costa Rica, Final Report for the Spencer Foundation." *Cultural Practices of Literacy Study*. N.p., n.d. Web. 6 Mar. 2012.

———. *Other People's Words: The Cycle of Low Literacy*. Cambridge, MA: Harvard University Press, 1995. Print.

———. *Cultural Practices of Literacy: Case Studies of Language, Literacy, Social Practice, and Power*. Mahwah, NJ: Lawrence Erlbaum, 2007. Print.

Purcell-Gates, Victoria, Kristen Perry and Adriana Briseno. "Analyzing Literacy Practice: Grounded Theory to Model." *Research in the Teaching of English* 45.4 (2011): 439-458. Print.

Purcell-Gates, Victoria, Sophie C. Degener, Erik Jacobson and Marta Soler. . "Impact of Authentic Literacy Instruction on Adult Literacy Practices." *Reading Research Quarterly* 37 (2002): 70-92. Print.

Rannikmäe, Miia, Moonika Teppo, and Jack Holbrook. "Popularity and Relevance of Science Education Literacy: Using a Context-based Approach." *Science Education International*, 21.2 (2010): 116-125. *Education Research Complete*. Web. 20 Feb. 2012.

Roberts, Douglas A. "Scientific Literacy/Science Literacy." *Handbook of Research on Science Education*. Eds. Sandra K. Abell and Norman G. Lederman. Mahwah, NJ: Lawrence Erlbaum Associates, Publishers, 2007. 729-780. Print.

Rosolová, Kamila. "Literacy Practices in a Foreign Language: Two Cuban Immigrants." *Cultural Practices of Literacy: Case Studies of Language, Literacy, Social Practice, and Power.* Ed. Victoria Purcell-Gates. Mahwah, NJ: Lawrence Erlbaum, 2007. 99-114. Print.

Rudolph, John L. "Historical Writing on Science Education: A View of the Landscape." *Studies in Science Education* 44.1 (2008): 63-82. *Taylor & Francis Library.* Web. 20 Feb. 2012.

Shanahan, Timothy and Cynthia Shanahan. "Teaching Disciplinary Literacy to Adolescents: Rethinking Content Area Literacy." *Harvard Education Review* 78 (2008): 40–59. Print.

Shapin, Stephen. "Rarely Pure and Never Simple: Talking about Truth." *Configurations* 7 (1999): 1-14. *Project MUSE - Premium Collection.* Web. 22 Feb. 2012.

Sutherland, Dawn and Reg Dennick. "Exploring Culture, Language and the Perception of the Nature of Science." *International Journal of Science Education* 24.1 (2002): 1-25. (2002). *Taylor & Francis Library.* Web. 20 Feb. 2012.

Street, Brian. *Literacy in Theory and Practice.* Cambridge: Cambridge University Press, 1984. Print.

_____. *Social Literacies: Critical Approaches to Literacy in Development, Ethnography, and Education.* London: Longman, 1995. Print.

"Vancouver Case Studies of Underachieving School Communities." *Cultural Practices of Literacy Study.* N.p., n.d. Web. 6 Mar. 2012.

Velasco-Zárate, Kalinka. "Relationship between the Cultural Practices of Literacy and the Variability in Written L2 Spanish by Children Speakers of L1 Zapoteco (Valley) at the Elementary Level." *Cultural Practices of Literacy Study.* N.p., n.d. Web. 6 Mar. 2012.

Vygotsky, Lev S. *Mind in Society: The Development of Higher Psychological Processes.* Cambridge: Harvard University Press, 1978. Print.

Wellington, Jerry and Jonathan Osborne. *Language and Literacy in Science Education.* Philadelphia, PA: Open University Press, 2001. Print.

Yore, Larry D., Gay L. Bisanz, and Brian M. Hand. "Examining the Literacy Component of Science Literacy: 25 Years of Language and Science Research." *International Journal of Science Education* 25.6 (2003): 689–725. *Taylor & Francis Library.* Web. 20 Feb. 2012.

Yore, Larry D., Brian M. Hand, and Marilyn K. Florence. "Scientists' Views of Science, Models of Writing, and Science Writing Practices." *National Association for Research in Science Teaching Annual Meeting.* (2001).

Zhang, Gaoming. "Multiple Border Crossings: Literacy Practices of Chinese American Bilingual Families." *Cultural Practices of Literacy: Case Studies of Language, Literacy, Social Practice, and Power.* Ed. Victoria Purcell-Gates. Mahwah, NJ: Lawrence Erlbaum, 2007. 85-98. Print.

Author Bios

Dr. Adriana Briseño-Garzón is a postdoctoral fellow at the Centre for Cross Faculty Inquiry at the Faculty of Education, University of British Columbia, and she is also the Project Manager of the Cultural Practices of Literacy Study. Dr. Briseño-Garzón's research interests focus on the influence of social and cultural elements on people's learning experiences outside the classroom setting. She is also interested in the social nature of learning in museums, science education, the processes through which visitors create meaning across contexts of everyday life, and the relationships between museums and the construction of people's social identities.

Kristen H. Perry is an assistant professor in the department of Curriculum & Instruction at the University of Kentucky. Perry's work focuses primarily on literacy and culture in diverse communities, investigating everyday home/family and community literacy practices, particularly among African immigrant and refugee communities. She also researches educational opportunities with respect to ESL, literacy, and higher education for adult refugees. Perry is the recipient of the National Reading Conference's J. Michael Parker Award for research in adult literacy.

Victoria Purcell-Gates holds a Canada Research Chair in Early Childhood Literacy, Tier 1 at the Department of Language & Literacy at the University of British Columbia. She is the Principal Investigator of the Cultural Practices of Literacy Study. Her main research interests revolve around the ways in which people in communities value and practice literacy in all aspects of their lives. This includes texts, written symbol systems, purposes for reading and writing, attitudes and beliefs. Victoria also has designed multiple early literacy instruction initiatives that build on young children's linguistic, cognitive, cultural, and social models for reading and writing that they acquired within their home communities.

From the Book Review Editor's Desk

By Jim Bowman

This issue's keywords essay and reviews illustrate how, on the one hand, community literacy theories and practices are evolving to adapt to shifting cultural dynamics, especially on the level of administration and program design. Jennifer deWinter's discussion of the online community manager directs scholars of literacy to examine more closely the sophisticated language practices of gaming communities. Jessica Restaino and Laurie JC Cella's edited collection *Unsustainable: Re-Imagining Community Literacy, Public Writing, Service-Learning and the University*, reviewed by Jody Briones, offers a window into how experienced practitioners and theorists of community literacy have begun adjusting expectations, assessment practices, and everyday metaphors in order to effect meaningful change in communities long term—even, if necessary, at the expense of short-term gains. Swing big, goes the thinking. Realize, too, that programs that look and feel like failure, if they prioritize relationships with community partners, may eventually lead to something truly meaningful. Briones's review and deWinter's essay offer promising leads for scholars and administrators of community literacy to pursue—new ways to approach community, new communities to investigate.

The latter cluster of three books reviewed—*Cultural Practices of Literacy* by Victoria Purcell-Gates, *Local Literacies* by David Barton and Mary Hamilton and *Literacy in the Digital Age* by Richard W. Burniske—serve as important resources for scholars and teachers interested in more enduring conceptual understandings of cultural literacy, whether that be for purposes of ethnographic research, general literacy education, or teaching with technology. Our reviewers set out to assess the continuing relevance of such texts and have determined, for the most part, that they provide scholars and literacy educators with enduring, even essential frameworks. *Local Literacies*, for example, was re-released in 2012 and deemed a Routledge Linguistics Classic, a status that reviewer Charlotte Brammer and many others over the past two decades have found to be well-deserved. As new pathways in community literacy continue to emerge, it behooves us to continue building on the work of previous scholars, in an effort to remain conscious of the complicated dynamics at play among cultural literacies of home, work, school.

Community Management

Jennifer deWinter
Worcester Polytechnic Institute

Keyword Essay

Community literacy often engages with literacy practices—written, oral, visual, technological, social, and so forth—that occur and are scaffolded outside of traditional educational institutions. The writing done in community literacy projects, according to Peck, Flower, and Higgins, works to promote action and reflection while enabling people to work collaboratively and productively. In recognition of the multiple forms of literate practices and the types of community support that are needed and developed, a number of universities in the US have created community literacy programs. Carnegie Mellon University's Community Literacy Center, a notable example of this type of program, organizes the purposes and structural collaboration thusly: "At the Community Literacy Center (CLC) urban teens and adults, with the support of their Carnegie Mellon student mentors, use writing and public dialogue to take action and to address the dreams and problems of our urban neighborhoods. CLC writers produce powerful texts—petitions, plans, proposals, and newsletters" ("Hands On"). The benefit to both university students and community members is a collaborative workgroup dedicated to place-specific social action. Non-profit organizations have also formed, providing literacy support to particular communities, from Community Literacy Centers, Inc, which teaches adults to read, to Chicago's Open Books, which runs a volunteer bookstore and provides reading and writing programs.

In the above examples, the underpinning definition of community is spatially defined; thus, community literacy programs belong to a particular city, neighborhood, or group of people. The challenge is attending to opt-in communities that are not geographically defined—communities that form in large part because of Internet access and continuous involvement in online, virtual spaces rather than material locations. Centers, then, are replaced by forums, wikis, and avatar-mediated conversations, and in this environment, community center teachers and organizers are replaced by community managers, those people who work at the intersection between IP holders and players, mediating literate practices, mentoring new people, and working with players to effect changes to the system.

Community managers, as the title indicates, emerge from the business world in attempt to build and maintain brand loyalty through cultivating a dedicated community through social media and live social events. In discussing the evolution of the community manager, Michlmayr writes, "The benefits of communities and the need to facilitate and manage them have given rise to the community manager position. [… The community manager] ensures that there is a healthy community around the project, interacts with users, developers and other stakeholders, and facilitates organizational aspects of the project" (23). This suggests that community managers are shills for the business world; however, as Bacon explains in *The Art of Community: Building the New Age of Participation*, "community managers may well need to step outside the traditional boundaries of the business world. For a community manager to really build a rapport with the community, he needs to fundamentally be a member of that community and exhibit the culture of that community" (471). And in her *Forbes* article, Jennifer Grayeb defines the four pillars of community management as growth, engagement, listening, and improvement. The growth of the community is the growth of the brand, but aside from that, the latter three pillars are familiar to us in community literacy, for they are concerned with the sustainability of an engaged community.

In Massive Multiplayer Online Game (MMOG) communities, in particular, community managers have a prominent role because the number of members makes the environment potentially too large and alienating. According to Humphreys, the community manager position answers the particular challenges of online community sustainability. He writes: "The creation of subscription based virtual game worlds has generated the creation of communities. How are these communities to be managed? Do game participants hold all the rights of an ordinary offline citizen—the right to the same protections and freedoms? Is a publisher under any obligation to treat the game world community fairly?" (14). *World of Warcraft*, for example, is often cited as a community-building game, which accounts for its financial success and longevity. This is evidenced in numerous places: In "An Online Community as a New Tribalism: The World of Warcraft," Brignall and Van Valey argue, "Online communities offer individuals the ability to locate (at least in a virtual sense) and interact with other players who share a common identity or interests. WOW was explicitly designed to foster such socializing within the game." Indeed, it is this virtual socialization that has attracted attention from social scientists and literacy experts (see, for example, Nardi, *My Life as a Night Elf Priest*; Bainbridge, *The Warcraft Civilization: Social Science in a Virtual World*; Gee, *What Video Games Have to Teach Us About Learning and Literacy*; Squire, "Video-Game Literacy: A Literacy of Expertise"). Furthermore, as Gibbs et al. have discussed, the rich lives that people sustain in these games has given rise to in-game weddings and funerals, which reflect out-of-game events. Not only are people actively participating in their virtual communities, they are generating a tremendous amount of literacy-based artifacts. For example, the *World of Warcraft* wiki, or WoWWiki, is the second largest in the world (Wikipedia is the first), with over 80,000 articles, and 5 million people access it monthly (McGonigal). These varied creations of community and literacy practices have outpaced the original expectations or even control of the original game creators. Yet the IP holders are loath to quash this type of community building and community practice because the vitality of the online space requires these types of social interactions and knowledge creation to continue occurring.

The work of community managers is often invisible to the community it serves. According to the "Community Manager" page on the WoWWiki, "A Community Manager is a Blizzard Entertainment employee that monitors the World of Warcraft forums, acting as a liaison between the players and the developers, along with other community-related responsibilities." To this fairly simple definition, community manager Eyonix writes that his job entails disseminating information and providing feedback to the development team. "This feedback" he explains, "is gathered from numerous locations, which include but are certainly not limited to these forums, in-game chat, fan sites, guild sites, and third-party discussion forums." Further, he writes, "Beyond all of this, as a Community Manager I'm also here to moderate discussions, provide personal insight, offer humor, spotlight community related items, and silently absorb much of what our players are expressing and feeling." Thus, while Eyonix and other community managers participate and guide players, edit work written in public forums, and teach new players how to play, a vast majority of their work around players is simply listening and reading. Based on the garnered information, they are able to go back to developers, who are interested in refining the in-game experience.

Community managers are not just hired and assigned to the role. In these types of dynamic communities, community managers emerge just as often as they are consciously created. In their article "The Uses of Multimedia: Three Digital Literacy Case Studies," Hartley et al. discuss disruptions caused by digital literacy and the emerging role of the community manager as active literate agent:

> This attention-seeking and often competitive action can perhaps also be characterised as a type of Schumpeterian 'consumer entrepreneurialism', particularly because it is both creative and destructive. It creates knowledge, but this distributed network of professional and non-professional expertise also disrupts industrial-era modes of controlling and organising cultural production. This entrepreneurialism, as an emergent market, introduces growth, dynamism and change. A focus on this agency as a form of digital literacy exercised by creative consumer-citizens requires us to grapple with processes of the origination, adoption and retention of knowledge. (69)

The authors discuss the case of Alex Weekes, whose online fan participation in the community as a writer and knowledge builder transformed into professional community relations manager work. Similarly, Dan Gray's successful forum moderator ability brought him to the attention of the game company, and his digital literacy and community management transformed into a corporate job.

Community managers are expected to attend closely to the community (which is why active fans are often nurtured into this position), which feeds back into the development cycle, and the development cycle in computer games is invested in enhancing player experience and player community. In their case study "The Orchestrating Firm: Value Creation in the Video Game Industry," Gidhagen et al. note, "[a]lthough users actively help each other in solving problems and answering questions via the community, many developers have so called Community Managers employed who monitor the activities within the community and its different subforums." Their jobs go beyond simple monitoring activities, and their value is evidenced by the fact that some developers have hundreds of community managers. Through a number of activities, such as monitoring the community forums, reading social networking sites, visiting fan sites, and answering directed questions, "the Community Manager is a representative of the developer's way of attending to its users' requirements; they are to be considerate of, and pick up on, how gamers react to what the developer does. The role of a Community Manager therefore entails constant interaction and communication with users, especially with those users having been given the role of moderator in the community." And this constant interaction, according to Ruggles et al., is predicated on trust: "In order to build trust, players must feel that their issues are being heard and not being ignored, and that the commitments made to them by the developer are being fulfilled. Developers must ensure that they are communicating changes being made in the game and what the plans are for the future to the community (Company C)" (122).

Such feedback loops are not merely one way—from developer to consumer—but act to bring community players into the community of development as active co-creators. This, in turn, enables the participatory community to invest in the longitudinal sustainability and success of the community. For example, Jeppesen and Molin argue in "Consumers as Co-Developers: Learning and Innovation Outside the Firm," consumer communities generate innovation through their needs, ideas, and critiques, and the community manager can help to sustain a critical mass of people, enough so that the community is stable, and then translate community feedback to businesses. This is easily seen in computer game development, as Banks describes in both "Co-Creative Expertise: Auran Games and Fury—A Case Study" and his co-written article with Potts entitled "Co-Creating Games: A Co-Evolutionary Analysis." According to these two articles, the role of the active player as co-creator is powerful yet does not always fit into traditional industry practices. However, players and community managers are active participants in the community and know their informational, literate, or gamic needs. Banks reports that the community managers he talked with became frustrated with the development team and its lack of response to player feedback. The development team then became frustrated with players and their lack of development knowledge. According to Banks, "This problem and challenge of coordinating often competing and divergent if not incommensurable forms of expertise in the design decision-making process gets us to the core dilemma of distributed expertise networks" (10). And at the heart of these distributed expertise networks is the community manager, which explains the defensive position that Eyonix takes when he writes, "I wrote this post primarily because I've seen threads requesting clarification on what my role within the company was, and in general see a great deal of expectation surrounding the opinion of what I should be doing, and how I'm failing."

The community "centers" or sites in which community managers participate are difficult to pinpoint; like so much on the internet, community participation is dispersed and sometimes protected. In computer games, such as *World of Warcraft*, literate practices occur in game, in developer-created forums, and in game-specific wikis such as the WoWWiki. People come together in these sites to share their stories, mentor one another, and ask for help. However, in addition to these business-controlled centers, players will develop their own fan websites, Facebook pages, Twitter accounts, blogs, and online file sharing sites to disseminate fan fiction and machinima (cinematic shorts produced with a computer game engine). These exist in parallel to the codified developer-supported communities, and are equally important in maintaining a sense of community and also enabling the experience of the game to penetrate non-gaming life through alternative forms of participation. And this is important to mention in a keywords essay on community managers because community managers must also participate in these other venues of community action and respond to the types of information and action happening in non-corporate channels. Only through doing so does the community manager belong to the community at large rather than the institutionalized community.

The community manager, in the way that it is employed by business and gaming communities, seems in one sense to be a world away from community literacy and the situated knowledges of community practice. However, community managers are a response to the formation of digital communities, and oftentimes, digital communities overlay physical communities—made easier with smartphones and mobile Internet technologies. Indeed, De Cindio and Peraboni see the facilitative role of community managers, not in computer games, but in grassroot movements and community actions. In their article "Design Issues for Building Deliberative Digital Habitats," De Cindio and Peraboni write:

> The Galateo [code of conduct] brings along with it the need to choose a trusted person committed to let the Galateo be observed: this is the role of the community manager. Rather then being a censor in charge of disapproving messages that fail to comply with the Galateo, or a policeman who bans participants, s/he plays the role of the person who helps participants to state their ideas in fair and civil fashion. Thanks to this work s/he is recognized as a digital communication expert who supports less skilled participants (public officers, politicians, elected representatives as well as generic citizens) in learning and facing with the dynamics typical of the online environments.

The community manager, in this deliberative, social action situation, acts as a facilitator, a mentor in digital communication, and a guide in digital forums (those metaphoric Roman places for public discourse).

What we learn from the literature of community managers is the need to find all of the digital expressions of a singly defined community and bring those expressions into a coherent narrative to a particular end or need. It is no surprise that the business world created a position called "community manager" as they attempt to harness the consumer under the umbrella of certain brands. It is also of no surprise that computer games coopted the community manager to extend the formation of communities and provide a gamic experience that responds to community desires. What the final citation in this essay points to is the potential to learn from the efforts of community managers, who 1) mobilize dispersed and apparently disparate groups of people who are bound together by common needs and civic engagements and 2) find in those groups a narrative that brings them together. A community manager is, above all else, invested as an active member of a community and is interested in distilling hundreds, sometimes thousands of voices into clear themes and passing those onto the people who ostensibly serve those particular communities.

Works Cited

Bacon, Jono. *The Art of Community: Building the New Age of Participation*, 2nd ed. Sebastopol, CA: O'Reilly Media, 2012.
Bainbridge, William Sims. *The Warcraft Civilization: Social Science in a Virtual World*. Cambridge, MA: The MIT P, 2010.
Banks, John. "Co-Creative Expertise: Auran Games and Fury—A Case Study." *Media International Australia: Incorporating Culture and Policy*, 130 (Feb. 2009): 77-89.
_____, and Jason Potts. "Co-Creating Games: A Co-Evolutionary Analysis." *New Media and Society* 12.2 (2010): 253-70.
Brignall, Thomas W., and Van Valey, Thomas L. "An Online Community as a New Tribalism: The World of Warcraft." *Proceedings of the 40th Hawaii International Conference on System Sciences*, 2007.
"Community Manager." *WoWWiki*. 2013. Web. 4 Aug. 2013.
De Cindio, Fiorella, and Cristian Peraboni. "Design Issues for Building Deliberative Digital Habitats." *From e-Participation to Online Deliberation*, Proceedings of the 4th International Conference on Online Deliberation, OD2010. Leeds, UK, 30 June - 2 July, 2010. 41-52.
Eyonix. "My Role." *WoW BlueTracker*. 14 July 2006. Web. 4 August 2013.
Gee, James Paul. *What Video Games Have to Teach Us About Learning and Literacy*. NY: Palgrave Macmillan, 2003.
Gibbs, Martin, Joji Mori, Michael Arnold, and Tamara Kohn. "Tombstones, Uncanny Monuments and Epic Quests: Memorials in World of Warcraft." *Game Studies*, 12. Retrieved October 3, 2012 from <http://gamestudies.org/1201/articles/gibbs_martin>
Gidhagen, Mikael, Oscar Persson Ridell, and David Sörhammar. "The Orchestrating Firm: Value Creation in the Video Game Industry." Emerald 21 (2011): 1-16.
Grayeb, Jennifer. "The 4 Pillars of Community Management." *Forbes*. 25 Dec. 2012. Web. 3 Aug. 2013.
"Hands On Community Literacy: Backfiles 1986-1996 from the Community Literacy Center." N.d. Web. 3 August 2013.
Hartley, John, Kelly McWilliam, Jean E. Burgess, and John A. Banks. "The Uses of Multimedia: Three Digital Literacy Case Studies." *Media International Australia: Incorporating Culture and Policy* 128 (2008): 59-72.

Humphreys, Sal. "Productive Users, Intellectual Property and Governance: The Challenges of Computer Games." *Media and Arts Law Review* 10.4 (2005): 299-310.

Jeppesen, Lars Bo, and Måns J. Molin "Consumers as Co-developers: Learning and Innovation Outside the Firm." *Technology Analysis and Strategic Management* 15:3 (2003): 363-83.

McGonigal, Jane. "Gaming Can Make a Better World." *TED: Ideas Worth Spreading.* Feb. 2010. Web. Aug. 4, 2013.

Michlmayr, Martin. "Community Management for Open Source Projects." *Upgrade: The European Journal for the Informatics Professional.* X.3 (June 2009): 22-26.

Nardi, Bonnie. *My Life as a Night Elf Priest: An Anthropological Account of World of Warcraft.* Ann Arbor: U of Michigan P, 2010.

"Open Books." 2013. Web. 3 August 2013.

Peck, W., Flower, L., & Higgins, L. "Community Literacy." *College Composition and Communication.* 46.2 (1995): 199-222.

Ruggles, Christopher, Greg Wadley, and Martin R. Gibbs. "Online Community Building Techniques Used by Video Game Developers." *Entertainment Computing*—ICEC 2005. 4th International Conference, Sanda, Japan, September 19-21, 2005: 114-25.

Squire, Kurt D. "Video-Game Literacy: A Literacy of Expertise." *Handbook of Research on New Literacies.* New York: Routledge, 2010. 635-70.

WoWWiki. 2013. Web. 5 August 2013.

Unsustainable: Re-Imagining Community Literacy, Public Writing, Service-Learning and the University

Restaino, Jessica and Laurie JC Cella, eds.
Lanham, MD: Lexington Books, 2013. 275 pp.

Reviewed by Jody A. Briones
Texas A&M University-Kingsville

In *Unsustainable: Re-Imagining Community Literacy, Public Writing, Service-Learning and the University*, the collection's authors address community and university factors that contribute to unsustainable civic and service-learning projects. In light of the shortcomings outlined in these projects, the collection advocates for a more flexible way of defining and assessing sustainability, something Paula Mathieu calls for in *Tactics of Hope*, a community literacy text that is significantly referenced throughout *Unsustainable*. In *Tactics of Hope*, Mathieu states that all sustainable projects are unpredictable; therefore, service-learning leaders and practitioners must create alternative visions of projects as the needs and circumstances of these projects change, including nontraditional assessment methodologies. University-led civic and service-learning projects are traditionally assessed based on  the sustainability of the project and the successful completion of university goals (17). *Tactics of Hope* encourages nontraditional assessment methodologies that focus on the collaborative processes and personal relationships formed between community and university, meaning projects can be "unsustainable" but still be successes because of the positive relationships formed. It is this concept of nontraditional assessment of sustainability that *Unsustainable* advocates for—finding successes in "unsustainable" civic and service-learning projects.

In Part I, "Short-Lived Projects, Long-Lived Value," contributing authors discuss factors that caused their respective university-based service-learning projects to prematurely end, and, in some cases, how projects continued, in altered form, when university sponsorship ended. The section begins with Mathieu's "After Tactics, What Comes Next?," which picks up where *Tactics of Hope* leaves off. In Chapter 1, Mathieu updates readers that the three-way community partnership of Boston College, Sandra's Lodge (a Boston-based homeless shelter), and *Spare Change News* (a Boston street newspaper written by the homeless and low-income) she discussed in *Tactics of Hope* was unsustainable after it lost significant funding and detached from the academic course to which it was initially linked. Although the project was unsustainable, Mathieu does not view the project a failure. She ends the chapter by emphasizing the necessity of an evolutionary ideology and methodology of civic and service-learning projects: "projects can end, sometimes abruptly; they can (and perhaps should) become institutionalized as ongoing university-community partnerships; they can change into other projects or other configurations of partnership, or they might end and perhaps begin again" (17). The three remaining chapters in Part I each describe a civic or service-learning project that would become unsustainable due to institutional/community power differentials. The crux of the problem for faculty is "working with the system without becoming of the system" (36), as Paul Feigenbaum, Sharayna Douglas, and Maria Lovett explain in Chapter 2. The collapse of this dichotomy, in its various forms, hinders the sustainability of a project.

In Part II, "Community Literacy, Personal Contexts," junior faculty discuss the dichotomous relationship of tenure and promotion assessment and the commitment to community engagement projects. Chapters 5 and 6 explore the contradictions of institutional mission statements of public service (intentions) and the low value public service projects are given in tenure and promotion assessment (actions). It is for this reason Donnelly recommends junior faculty not spearhead service-learning or civic engagement projects. Instead, Donnelly recommends junior faculty participate in an already existing project, letting senior faculty take the lead or waiting until after tenure and promotion to establish a service-learning or civic engagement project. However, not establishing or participating in sustainable projects is a lost opportunity for professional marketability. To deal with the lack of long-term sustainable projects, Karen Johnson, in Chapter 7, advocates for mobile sustainability, which is the consistency of a service, no matter the location or population. Like Deans and Donnelly, Johnson explains how her lack of power as an adjunct and the multiple institutional moves she made to accept better institutional offers limited her opportunities for long-term sustainable projects: "mobile sustainability for service initiatives was my only option as an adjunct because I lacked power to enact change and the institutional knowledge to effectively build an institutionalized program" (154-55). Invoking Mathieu's ideology that sustainable projects are unpredictable as their needs evolve, Johnson emphasizes that mobile sustainability forces acculturation as project needs and methodologies are consistently being (re)assessed.

Part III, "Pedagogy," suggests alternative theoretical frameworks for enacting and assessing service-learning projects. For example, in Chapter 9, Hannah Ashley invokes border theory by using Gloria Anzaldúa's concept of *mestiza* consciousness, an in-between, third space subject position, to describe the subject position of writing center mentors. More specifically, Ashley presents the idea of the writing center as a third space "birthing center," where writing mentors occupy *mestiza* consciousness as students' "literacy dulas" (179). As literacy dulas, writing "[m]entors work together with writers in the writers' own interests, to find productive locations and to birth productive just-outsider discourses" (192), what Ashley refers to as mentor and mentee "exchanges in interstitial moments" (182). The importance of relationships is also the focus of Chapter 8, which emphasizes the progressive relationship building within service-learning projects amongst academic institutions, participating communities, faculty, and students. In Chapter 8, Lorelei Blackburn and Ellen Cushman argue that relationship building amongst the entities that create the service-learning projects "needs to be woven throughout the entire process of developing [and delivering] teaching curricula...as well as in evaluation and assessment" of the project (163). Blackburn and Cushman state that the sustainability of a project depends on the relationship of the players: if the relationship between the players is good, then sustainability of the project is likely; if the relationship between the players is strained, then the project is more likely to be unsustainable. Therefore, Blackburn and Cushman argue that the material out-put the project creates and the relationships built during the project should both be considered the "products" of the project (171).

Part IV, "Calls for Transnational Sustainability," investigates how diverse forms of rhetoric can be used to sustain communities, specifically diasporic ethnic groups within the U.S. In Chapter 10, Elenore Long discusses how Gambian-Americans and members of the Nipmuck tribe in Massachusetts use transgressive technai, in the form of rhetorical intervention and invention, to create "new paths, new outcomes" (205) for their respective communities, creating a transformative sustainability of culture. Similarly, Jennifer Clifton, in Chapter 11, reflects on the negative and positive transgressive effects rhetoric, as stochastic art, has had on Sudanese refugees in Phoenix. Although both Clifton and Long advocate for the sustainability of these communities, Clifton argues, "sustainability is neither a goal nor something to be celebrated except as either of these serve the rhetorical purposes of pursuing the health of the communities we engage with" (230). In other words, the needs of the community must always be of priority.

The conclusion by collection co-editor Jessica Restaino and the afterword by community-based learning scholar Eli Goldblatt are both calls-to-action for a revisioning of sustainability projects based on university/community partnerships. Restaino states, "The call...needs to be for a more radical refiguring of what university/community collaborations might look like and how they can be valued" (253). She also argues that universities need to place a higher value on civic and service-learning projects to encourage more academics to create or participate in these sustainable initiatives. Goldblatt, on the other hand, argues that to participate in a civic or service-learning project out of professional obligation or personal guilt "is ultimately selfish and its products unsustainable" (264) because of the lack of sincerity. Goldblatt encourages "to act out of compassion" (264), which, when coupled with allegiances and partnerships also acting out of compassion, makes positive change inevitable and sustainable.

Unsustainable asks the target audience of academicians to reevaluate how they define, enact, and assess civic and service-learning projects and sustainability. Placed in a larger discussion, this collection creates a dialogue with Ellen Cushman's "Sustainable Service Learning Programs," Christian Weisser's *Moving beyond Academic Discourse: Composition Studies and the Public Sphere*, Eli Goldblatt's *Because We Live Here:*

Sponsoring Literacy beyond the College Curriculum, and of course, Paula Mathieu's *Tactics of Hope: The Public Turn in English Composition*, a text largely referenced throughout this collection. Unique to this collection, however, and its main strength, is the focus on "unsuccessful," or unsustainable, civic and service-learning projects. Authors explain the "what went wrong" aspects of their unsustainable projects to (re)evaluate the definition, enactment, and assessment of sustainability with more fluidity and flexibility.

A misfire in this collection is the incorporation of Border Theory (*mesitza* consciousness—Chapter 9), Maternal Theory (literacy dula—Chapter 9), and Greek mythology (techne/chronos/kairos—Chapters 10 and 11). Although these are relevant and valued theories and discussions, these chapters feel disconnected from the rest of the collection because of their heavy reliance on theoretical abstractions instead of concrete examples, like most chapters in the collection. These chapters belong in a more theoretically-based collection.

Overall, *Unsustainable* is a must-read for all faculty and university administrators who engage in civic and service-learning projects. Although it does not provide specific solutions to troubled projects and their inevitable unsustainability, this collection is an invaluable resource on how to create or revise institutional civic and service-learning programs. Furthermore, *Unsustainable* should also be required reading in graduate programs that emphasize sustainability because it forces readers to question the definition of sustainability and how it should be enacted and assessed.

Cultural Practices of Literacy: Case Studies of Language, Literacy, Social Practice, and Power

Purcell-Gates, Victoria, ed.
Mahwah, NY: Lawrence Erlbaum, 2007. Print. $46.95

Reviewed by Kelly A. Concannon Mannise

Nova Southeastern University, Fort Lauderdale, FL.

In *Cultural Practices of Literacy* Victoria Purcell-Gates argues that school-based literacy instruction does not necessarily transfer into the literacy practices in individuals' everyday lives. Drawing from a theoretical framework that reveals how literacy is a social practice, Purcell-Gates constructs an edited collection where contributors to this volume are part of the Cultural Practices of the Literacy Studies (CPLS) team. The collection disrupts an assumed correlation between direct English-based literacy instruction in schools and the literacies practiced by members of traditionally marginalized groups in everyday contexts. Contributors to this collection employ ethnographic methodologies to provide a careful and detailed account of participants' uses of literacy within and outside of the classroom. They present complex accounts of individuals' literacy practices, indicating how power is always embedded in the use of reading, writing, and speaking, as many scholars invested in "non-traditional" literacies have long explored (See Albright, Ball; Cushman; Barton and Hamilton; Brandt; Brodkey; Gee).

The first chapter affords readers with the theoretical and methodological basis for the Cultural Practices of Literacy Studies (CPLS) study. In "Complicating the Complex," Purcell-Gates discusses how each chapter follows a standard protocol that explicitly reveals contributors' locations and relationships to participants. This move serves as a general introduction to each chapter, which is followed by a description of the historical and/or cultural contexts where literacy practices emerge. The framework informs all studies in the collection; Purcell-Gates intends to encourage readers to identify patterns across studies and make more generalized claims about the relationships amongst schooling, literacy, and literacy development. To that end, Purcell-Gates gathers information about the material conditions through which individuals participate in literacy events—emphasizing the extent to which literacy is a social practice—while presenting substantial evidence for an understanding of how hegemony, power, and domination affect the uses and representations of literacies (15-17).

The collection is invested in changing the ways that certain literacy practices are valued over others. Purcell-Gates argues that this collection responds to a need to "paint a picture of literacy as multiple and social"; therefore, she optimistically positions this project as one that presents a global range of the ways individuals use literacy practices (ix). Contributors seek to provide a more global understanding of contested uses of literacy in spaces not fully explored by researchers; however, their commitment to these outcomes and their use of an ethnographic methodology may limit this outcome.

The collection falls short in providing a full account of the *most valued* literacy practices of participants. Because of the large scope of this project, it is difficult to make substantial claims about patterns in literacy use in such different populations. The collection provides snapshots of school-based literacy practices as well as those performed outside of the traditional classroom, where a small number of individuals serve as representatives of a particular group. This need for consistency across chapters in the CLPS study—along with multiple exigencies to establish historical and cultural contexts of particular rhetorical situations where literacy practices are employed—makes it more difficult for contributors to create substantial claims about the social nature of literacy of a more global range of participants.

The collection is broken down into four sections. The beginning of the collection discusses how linguistic hegemony in the context of imperialism is demonstrated through the lives of both Puerto Rican farmers and Botswana students. In this first portion, "Language, Literacy, and Hegemony," participants reflect on their literacy practices and produce detailed accounts of how they use English and their respective native languages at work, in schools, and in the home. Contributors address the larger cultural attitude that English is needed for access into a global economy because they highlight how participants are rhetorically savvy in gaining access to information and resources while not fully assimilating into the dominant culture. For example, in chapter 3 "Language and Literacy Issues in Botswana," Annah Molosiwa conducts a series of interviews with individuals from Botswana who discuss how they negotiate both English and their native language. Participants explain how they use English when reading printed text, yet they indicate that oral literacies are utilized in their homes (47-48). Molosiwa's contribution raises questions about the nature of schooling for Botswana students because their reflections of their literacy practices reveal a clear division between home, on the one hand, and religion, school, and work on the other. Therefore, she argues that additional research on the literacy practices of non-native speakers of English should consider literacy acquisition in the home because before students reach school their exposure to print literacy is minimal (53-54).

Both studies in this section emphasize how historical struggles over power are reflected through current uses of literacy. Participants reveal how they are cognizant of the ways that using English in certain contexts produces favorable results. This first section makes visible and valuable the use of literacy by non-native speakers of English and emphasizes how individuals make clear and distinct choices about using their non-native language. Purcell-Gates pushes the boundaries of location (working with individuals outside of the United States) and draws attention to participants' awareness of the effects of using the dominant language to accomplish their goals.

While the previous section addresses how language is negotiated in the context of linguistic domination and oppression, the next section mobilizes these conversations by using the theme of immigration as a point of entry. In "The Immigrant Experience: Languages, Literacies, and Identities," contributors focus on how country of origin, native language, and purpose for immigration factor into the literacy practices of Sudanese, Chinese, and Cuban immigrants. They reveal how immigrants draw from past experiences—including their experiences with family members—to successfully participate in contexts that require the use of English.

For example, in chapter 5, "Multiple Border Crossing: Literacy Practices of Chinese American Bilingual Families," Gaoming Zhang examines the literacy practices of two Chinese American bilingual families to emphasize the relationships amongst school-based literacies and the impact of family support on overall literacy development. Unlike some of the previous studies in this collection, Zhang's case studies indicate that school-based instruction—both in English as well as Chinese-based weekend schooling—impacted literacy practices outside of school. School literacy was transferred to self-motivated learning: "what was learned in school was supplemented and applied to after-school, self-motivated activities" (93). Therefore, this study indicates that in some cases, school literacies do make their way into the practices that students engage in outside of the classroom; however, Zhang resists a one-to-one correlation by drawing attention to the role of family in providing support for literacy practices (96).

In this section, notable patterns of literacy use are identified through the concept of "immigrant", which serves to bind many of these participants together, even as there are notable differences in their experiences as immigrants in the United States. Even as contributors to the collection argue that certain factors like family, access to resources, and explicit support in schools and at home directly affect the successes of the "immigrant," there is a clear tension between directly describing their literacy practices in the US, their past experiences, and finally, the overall historical contexts that produce these literacies. The scope of this section makes it difficult to provide a more detailed account of the different literacy practices by individuals within these respective groups.

The remainder of the book is grounded in the context of the US classroom and is heavily invested in making visible the literacy practices of "at-risk" students. Participants in this section reflect on literacy practices in different domains of their lives and shed light on the fact that boundaries between domains of literacy use are fluid. In the first portion, "Literacies in and out of School and on the Borders," contributors explore the borders between in-school and out-of-school literacies. Research in this section provides a strong case for taking additional time to work with participants to ascertain how they understand the significance of literacy in their everyday lives. This particular section provides an effective model for creating meaningful relationships with participants. For example, in Chapter 8 "Literacy and Choice: Urban Elementary

Students' Perceptions of Links Between Home, School, and Community Literacy Practices," Jodene Kersten works with fifth graders, who were invited to aid in the process of documenting their out-of-school literacy practices with disposable cameras (134-46). Students discuss how they succeed using literacy in contexts out of schools. Results indicate that participants are cognizant of the ways that their literacy practices at home differ from those valued in a school setting, thereby placing responsibility on the schools to more directly take into account the literacy practices and values that the children bring to the classroom (150-53).

This section also provides a glimpse of the literacy practices of "mainstream" students. In "School and Home: Contexts for Conflict and Agency," for example, Chad O'Neil outlines significant turning points in writing tutors' understandings of literacy; he emphasizes how they see their families' role in cultivating this literacy (174-75). Each participant's account of literacy draws attention to the school's role in identifying out-of-school literacies as valuable in their lives (178). This chapter provides a backdrop to understand the literacy practices of students who successfully work in a university climate; however, this chapter works as an anomaly against the contributions that precede it. Even as this work may enhance our overall understanding of literacy as a social practice, the chapter is indicative of scope evident throughout the collection, as conducting research with two college writing tutors on their literacy practices begins to note strong patterns in "mainstream" users of literacy.

This collection is a wake-up call for both educators and policy-makers because it establishes a theoretical framework for responsibly gathering research about literacy practices outside of the classroom. Indeed, contributors do demand that future research on individuals' literacy practices must be done in order to maintain an understanding of literacy as social. However, the relationship between the work in this collection and the ultimate goals for future work in literacy studies walks a fine line. The collection provides a glimpse of the uses of literacy through a description of a limited number of case studies. However, contributors still create a serious call-to-action for other scholars interested in literacy, educational policies, and linguistics to contribute to these conversations by providing their own in-depth studies of people on both a local and global level.

Works Consulted

Albright, James, and Allan Luke, ed. *Pierre Bourdieu and Literacy Education*. New York: Routledge, 2008. Print.

Ball, Arnetha F., and Ted Lardner. *African American Literacies Unleashed: Vernacular English and the Composition Classroom*. Urbana, IL: National Council of Teachers of English, 2005. Print.

Barton, David and Mary Hamilton. *Local Literacies: Reading and Writing in One Community*. London: Routledge, 1998. Print.

Brandt, Deborah. *Literacy in American Lives*. Cambridge, MA: Cambridge UP, 2001. Print.

Brodkey, Linda. *Writing Permitted in Designated Areas Only*. Minneapolis: U Minnesota P, 1996. Print.

Cushman, Ellen. *The Struggle and the Tools: Oral and Literate Strategies in an Inner City Community*. Albany, NY: State U of New York P, 1998. Print.

Gee, James Paul. *Social Linguistics and Literacies: Ideology in Discourses*. 2nd ed. Bristol, PA: Taylor and Francis, 1996. Print.

Local Literacies: Reading and Writing in One Community
David Barton and Mary Hamilton.
London: Routledge, 2012. Print. Routledge Linguistics Classics. 265 pp. plus appendices. $49.95

Reviewed by Charlotte Brammer
Samford University

"Literacy is primarily something people do." This clause is no less profound today than when David Barton and Mary Hamilton used it to open *Local Literacies: Reading and Writing in One Community* in 1998. Routledge re-published the text in 2012 as part of the Routledge Linguistics Classics, and rightly so. As Deborah Brandt notes in the new foreword for the text, *Local Literacies* "changed the direction of literacy research, providing overwhelming material evidence of how local contexts matter to the achievement of literacy and how cultural practices give literacy its point and meaning" (xiii). Barton and Hamilton were clear in their purpose "of challenging discourses of literacy that are dominant and simplifying"  (xiv) and in explicating their ethnographic methods. Barton and Hamilton had three goals in this research project: to describe literacy practices in a particular community, explore literacy as a method of sense-making, and examine literacy's relationship to quality of life. The intentional ethnographic methods they employed allowed them to achieve each of these goals.

The text contains fourteen chapters plus an afterword, divided among three sections. Part I, which holds chapters one through four, establishes the parameters and underlying theory that guides this foray into literacy. Chapter One: Understanding Literacy as Social Practice has become something of a mainstay in literacy research for the six propositions that Barton and Hamilton aver as foundational to their approach to literacy. First, literacy means social practices: "Literacy practices are the general cultural ways of utilizing written language which people draw upon in their lives" (6). Second, literacy is context dependent, meaning that different contexts or "domains" require or hold or perhaps generate different literacies and literacy expectations. Power is key to literacies, which ones are practiced, privileged, visible, and dominant. Fourth, literacy practices are richly layered in that they are "purposeful and embedded in broader social goals and cultural practices" (6). History is part of the layering of literacy practice. Traditions, ideology, and culture feed the literacy practices of any community, and such practices "are as fluid, dynamic and changing as the lives of the societies of which they are a part" (12). Finally because societies are not static, literacy practices must be dynamic. New literacy practices must be learned "through processes of informal learning and sense making as well as formal education and training" (12). These six propositions guide Barton and Hamilton's framework for exploring and interpreting the literacy practices of a particular community in Lancaster, England, in 1990.

Chapters two and three are devoted exclusively to preparing the reader to understand and appreciate the literacy practices of the Lancaster community. In adhering to the carefully defined propositions of literacy, Barton and Hamilton devote considerable effort to explaining how literacy has developed in Lancaster, the kinds of influences that have shaped literacy practices since the Romans ruled the area (Chapter 2) and the state of literacy practices, to the extent there is moment of stasis, in Lancaster, 1990 (Chapter 3). The descriptions, photos, and maps from Lancaster, 1990, document a time prior to mass use of computers and portable computing devices, but the lessons learned continue to resonate. Information in these two chapters is frequently referenced in subsequent chapters.

In addition to detailing a rich description of literacy, Barton and Hamilton's *Local Literacies* is known for its exemplary ethnographic methods, which are carefully outlined in Chapter 4. This particular chapter is a must read for any student or researcher interested in learning ethnography. Ethnographies take place in "real-world settings" and offer authentic and "holistic" descriptions of the events and practices found in those settings. Ethnographers employ various methods; in this study, Barton and Hamilton interviewed adults at a local college, surveyed the "Springside" (pseudonym) community in Lancaster, used case studies of a number of individuals, and collaborated with community members to review interview data, observations, and interpretations. Interpretation is central to ethnographic research, and Barton and Hamilton were very careful in describing their process of analysis and interpretation, including the training and reconciliation of data coding. They intended and succeeded in "mak[ing] these examples of everyday literacy intelligible within the framework of cultural practices and social theory which [they] adopted, producing classifications, conceptual tools and theoretical explanations which can be used to extend understandings of literacy in other contexts" (72-73). One need look no further than Google Scholar to see that this text has been cited at least 1,620 times and to understand that Barton and Hamilton were successful in this goal.

Part II, which contains chapters five through eight, feature rich descriptions of four individuals from Springside and reveal the depth and joy of qualitative research. The lives of Harry, Shirley, June, and Cliff (all pseudonyms) reveal the everyday literacies of average folks in a working-class community, literacies that are as varied as the individuals and yet share some commonalities. These descriptions of individual struggles and successes are similar to those written by Shirley Brice Heath's *Ways with Words* in terms of making more literacy practices visible, practices that might otherwise remain hidden.

In Part III, Barton and Hamilton dig deeper into the literacy practices of Harry, Shirley, June, and Cliff within the context of the larger community, to identify a range of literacy practices, from reading habits to notions of morality and values embedded in literacy practices (Chapter 9), and patterns of practices, in terms of gendered practices as well as multilingual literacies (Chapter 10). They also interrogate the intersections and borderlands as well as the power structures that complicate those spaces where literacy practices happen (Chapters 11-13). Perhaps vernacular literacies are the most complicated spaces of literacy practices, and Barton and Hamilton discuss some of these complications in Chapter 14. According them, "vernacular literacies are in fact hybrid practices which draw on a range of practices from different domains" (247). In other words, the lines between literacy practices are permeable in that practices from one may, and frequently do, affect those in another area. For example, literacy practices and knowledge learned from participating in a hobby may influence and be influenced by literacy practices from work or school.

In brief, Barton and Hamilton's *Local Literacies* is a classic text on literacy and ethnography. It provides a solid framework that continues to move literacy studies forward.

Works Cited

Barton, David, and Mary Hamilton. *Local Literacies: Reading and Writing in One Community.* 1998. London: Routledge, 2012. Print.

Heath, Shirley Brice. *Ways with Words: Language, Life, and Work in Communities and Classrooms.* Cambridge: Cambridge UP, 1983. Print.

Literacy in the Digital Age, 2nd edition

Burniske, Richard W.
Thousand Oaks, CA: Corwin Press, 2008. $29.95.

Reviewed by Lilian Mina
Indiana University of Pennsylvania

In the digital age of computer technologies, writing teachers must often choose to either refurbish their classes and pedagogies with new technologies or risk losing their students' attention and interest. Teachers are required now more than ever before to make decisions to move away from the functional literacy that governed the education system in the U.S. and many countries for decades. Such changes create space for new forms of literacy our students desperately need to live and prosper in such a digitized world.

The title of Burniske's book can be quite misleading because it connotes that the book is about digital and computer literacy. In reality, this book makes its central argument that literacy in the digital age is not limited to computer or technical literacy; literacy is an umbrella concept that embraces a wide spectrum of literacies that emerged and became integral over time. This book presents these literacies and a computer-based approach to bringing each literacy to the writing class. The essence of the book is the literacies introduced, rather than computers or other technologies.

The book has two fundamental features: definitions and literacy challenges. This book provides working definitions of each type of literacy presented. These definitions establish a common ground for readers of varying experience with literacy theory. Burniske's definitions break down each literacy into a set of complementary passive and active skills and practices. For example, civil literacy is defined as "the ability to read, interpret, and respect the moral and ethical beliefs embraced by a particular social group and apply them in a responsible manner" (19). This definition does not stop at the passive skills of reading and understanding the beliefs of a given social group, but it enacts these skills in active application.

Literacy in the Digital Age also "serves as a philosophical guide while providing practical ideas for classroom practitioners" (2). These practical ideas come in the form of literacy challenges, or detailed activities that can be adopted and adapted to different classes, students, and contexts. One good example of these literacy challenges is in chapter 4 on personal literacy. The "Why List" literacy challenge (64 – 65) is an interesting and thought provoking activity that helps readers think critically about technology-related social beliefs and phenomena. Students are expected to generate their questions that they will answer later. This activity can be implemented in any class in which students are asked to write a research paper.

It shouldn't go without saying here that the technologies discussed in this book may not be the state-of-the-art ones that are available for teachers and scholars today to use and examine. This is due to the rapid leaps in social media and Web 2.0 technologies that happened after this book was initially published. For example, the book introduces activities for technologies like synchronous chat rooms, a technology that has evolved. Nevertheless, it is important to note that because the prime focus of the book is developing a wide range of literacies rather than examining new technologies, the book can still be of value to writing teachers, scholars, literacy specialists, historians, and curriculum designers. Writing teachers, for instance, can import many of the activities included in this book to some of the newer technologies available now, whereas scholars and historians may examine the evolution of literacy applications across different generations of technology. Media specialists, though, may not have the same degree of interest in the book, particularly if they are looking into newer forms of digital technology that are not present in this book.

The book is divided by literacy into eight short chapters. Each chapter deals with a different literacy and activities that can be applied in networked classrooms to develop this literacy in students. The systematic structure of chapters follows the following format: A short introduction of the literacy; A definition; Literacy challenges and/or case studies; Some explanatory thoughts. This makes it a handy source for teachers looking for activities, for literacy theorists looking for links between the literacy definitions and applications, and for scholars exploring rationales behind each activity.

The first chapter, "Media Literacy," lays the foundation to the literacies that follow in subsequent chapters. Burniske cautions teachers of the sheer enthusiasm that would make many of them jump into bringing all forms of literacy to their classes at once. He frames his media literacy definition with the rhetorical appeals (ethos, pathos, and logos) and uses this framework to extend computer literacy to become community literacy where all activities "require participation in the ancient art of persuasion that scholars of ancient Greece called rhetoric" (11). This approach provides a feasible way for teachers to link the small community of the classroom to the larger communities outside the classroom while allowing rhetoricians to investigate the links between media and rhetoric.

The second chapter, "Civil Literacy," is a call to teachers integrating any form of technology to teach students computer ethics in order to be responsible users of technology. The chapter posits collaborative learning as an essential civic literacy skill. Collaborative learning can be enacted in the form of students helping each other and their teacher with technology. Burniske brings the concept of civil literacy to a very practical level that students would appreciate and be able to practice.

The "Discourse Literacy" chapter deals with an essential form of literacy, the literacy of composing and presenting ourselves in online learning discourses. The biggest challenge, according to Burniske, is that "potential conflict exists between the expectations that students and teachers bring to these activities" (42). This chapter appeals to many audiences: it provides teachers with illustrations of example prompts to generate a thoughtful virtual discussion, it gives literacy theorists an approach to understanding and enacting discourse literacy in different contexts, and it stimulates a number of rules and directions for curriculum designers and teacher trainers to consider upon dealing with writing in virtual spaces.

Complementing the discourse literacy chapter, the personal literacy chapter focuses on students and how to make them go through the journey of self-reflection and awareness of their identity in an online community. Chapter five takes the inward-looking concept of personal literacy to the outward-looking concept of community literacy. Burniske presents a number of literacy challenges that aim to help students collaborate as connected members in an online community. Although the telecollaborative, sequential story activity is presented as a case study of community building, I could not think of it beyond a collaborative writing project that students may not perceive as a community-building one. Because this activity is implemented in sequence of emails, rather than exchanges and interaction, students may not feel they are part of a community the way they would do if they developed the same story on a discussion board or a blog. Needless to say that the book does not cover any Web 2.0 technologies due to its year of publication, which may limit its appeal to new media scholars, digital literacy theorists, cultural studies theorists, or teachers who incorporate such technologies in their writing classes.

Chapter six on "Visual Literacy" is a very interesting chapter that addresses evaluating websites and online resources through a number of innovative activities. Burniske borrows John Berger's argument that "The way we see things is affected by what we know or what we believe" (Berger as quoted in Burniske, 94). The central question in this chapter is "How might educators stimulate their students' critical literacy through the development of more astute visual literacy?" (94). The answer the chapter endorses is a sequential application of a rhetorical framework of evaluating websites. In this framework, ethos is represented in the creator and owner of the website, logos in argument and logical information presented on the site, and pathos in the use of visuals and textual arrangement. In reality, applying this framework involves different types of literacy, such as critical and personal literacy.

In a relatively short chapter on evaluative literacy, Burniske discusses developing students' critical judgment as an initial step toward improving their own writing. The chapter revolves around how the use of technology can "help students develop more evaluative literacy" (110). Through one literacy challenge and two case studies, the chapter demonstrates an electronic peer review of writing session, documenting and archiving online writing and learning activities through electronic portfolios, and keeping track of learning by using online learning records, respectively. The ideas and processes introduced in these activities can be adapted to more modern technologies teachers may use nowadays.

The pedagogical literacy chapter can be read as a personal message to all educators whether or not they integrate technology in their teaching. This is the only chapter that has no literacy challenges. This may be because pedagogical literacy is the teacher's central challenge. Through contemplating on their pedagogical literacy, teachers are capable of bringing all other literacies to their classes.

Burniske asks teachers who pay excessive attention to their materials at the expense of students to reverse the situation by intellectually challenging their students. He also challenges teachers who use technology for technology's sake, thinking that technology brings all positive influence to class, students, and teaching: "Telecomputing is not about computers. It's about educating our students, serving our communities, and improving our societies" (127).

Burniske's concluding statement remains true years after the book was published and as technology continues to entice and challenge teachers, literacy theorists, media specialists, and other communities of scholars. They all have to consider students as the core of education, students who will be responsible for advancing their communities and moving the whole society forwards. Therefore, students' mastery of the different literacies Burniske discusses in this book makes the book a valuable resource to different communities of readers.

PARLOR PRESS
EQUIPMENT FOR LIVING

Congratulations to These Award Winners!

GenAdmin: Theorizing WPA Identities in the Twenty-First Century

Colin Charlton, Jonikka Charlton, Tarez Samra Graban, Kathleen J. Ryan, & Amy Ferdinandt Stolley
Winner of the Best Book Award, Council of Writing Program Adminstrators (July, 2014)

Mics, Cameras, Symbolic Action: Audio-Visual Rhetoric for Writing Teachers
Bump Halbritter
Winner of the Distinguished Book Award from Computers and Composition (May, 2014)

New Releases

First-Year Composition: From Theory to Practice

Edited by Deborah Coxwell-Teague & Ronald F. Lunsford. 420 pages.
Twelve of the leading theorists in composition studies answer, in their own voices, the key question about what they hope to accomplish in a first-year composition course. Each chapter, and the accompanying syllabi, provides rich insights into the classroom practices of these theorists.

A Rhetoric for Writing Program Administrators

Edited by Rita Malenczyk. 471 pages.
Thirty-two contributors delineate the major issues and questions in the field of writing program administration and provide readers new to the field with theoretical lenses through which to view major issues and questions.

www.parlorpress.com

DEPAUL UNIVERSITY

DEPARTMENT OF WRITING, RHETORIC, & DISCOURSE

Master of Arts Degrees in
NEW MEDIA STUDIES
WRITING, RHETORIC, & DISCOURSE
with concentrations in
Professional & Technical Writing
Teaching Writing & Language

Graduate certificate in TESOL
Combined BA/MA in WRD

Bachelor of Arts in WRITING, RHETORIC, & DISCOURSE
Minor in **Professional Writing**

 facebook.com/DePaulWRD   @DePaulWRD

WRD.DEPAUL.EDU

www.ingramcontent.com/pod-product-compliance
Lightning Source LLC
Chambersburg PA
CBHW031324160426
43196CB00007B/662